A Collection of Artwork
Definitive edition 2015 - 2018

Josh Andrews

First published in 2018 in Great Britain by Achene UK Ltd, 2018

Copyright © 2018 by Josh Andrews.

This book is copyright under the Berne Convention.
No reproduction without permission.
All Rights Reserved.

The right of Josh Andrews to be identified as the author of this work has been asserted by him in accordance with sections 77 and 78 of the copyright, Designs and Patents Act, 1988.

ISBN-13: 978-1729654194

ISBN-10: 1729654193

The author and publishers have made all reasonable efforts to contact copyright holders for permission and apologize for any emissions or errors in the form of credits given. Corrections may be made to future printings.

A CIP catalogue record for this book is available from the British Library.

Interior and exterior design by Josh Andrews and Cara Jameson.

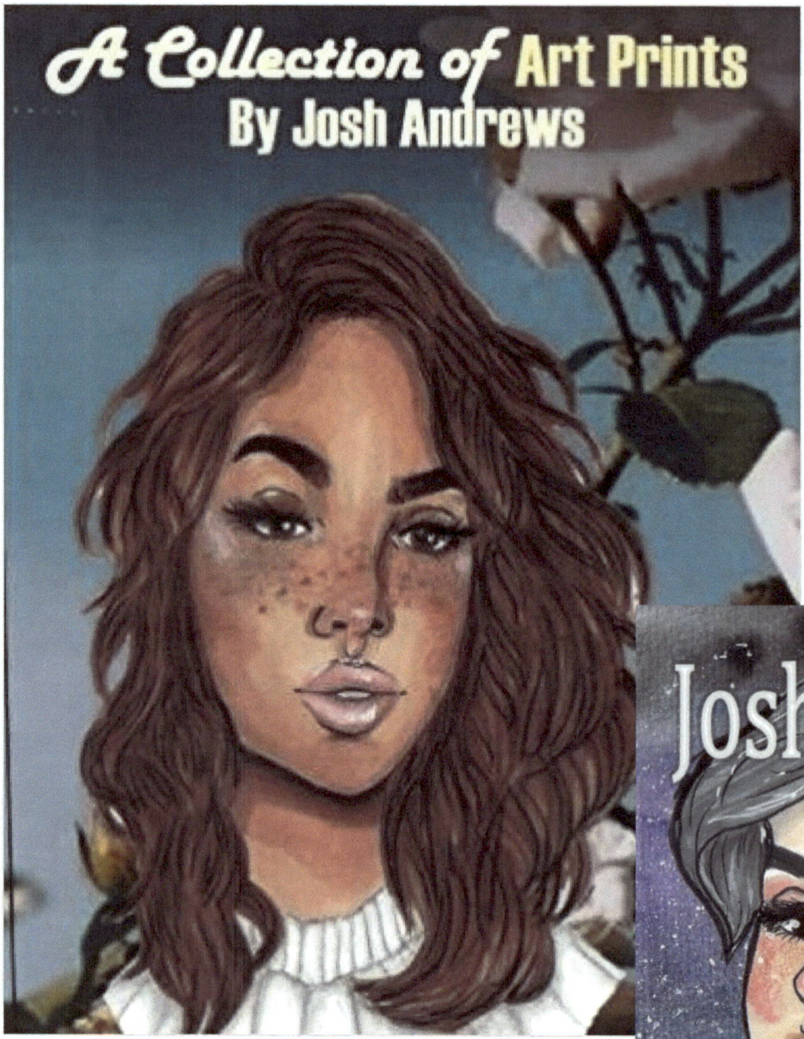

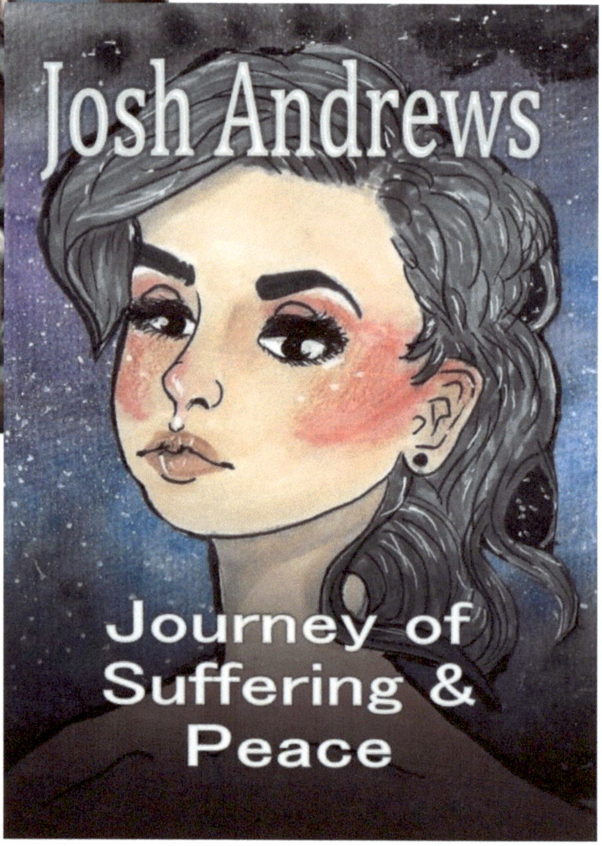

Thank you to all of you that bought either of my previous 2 books.

2015

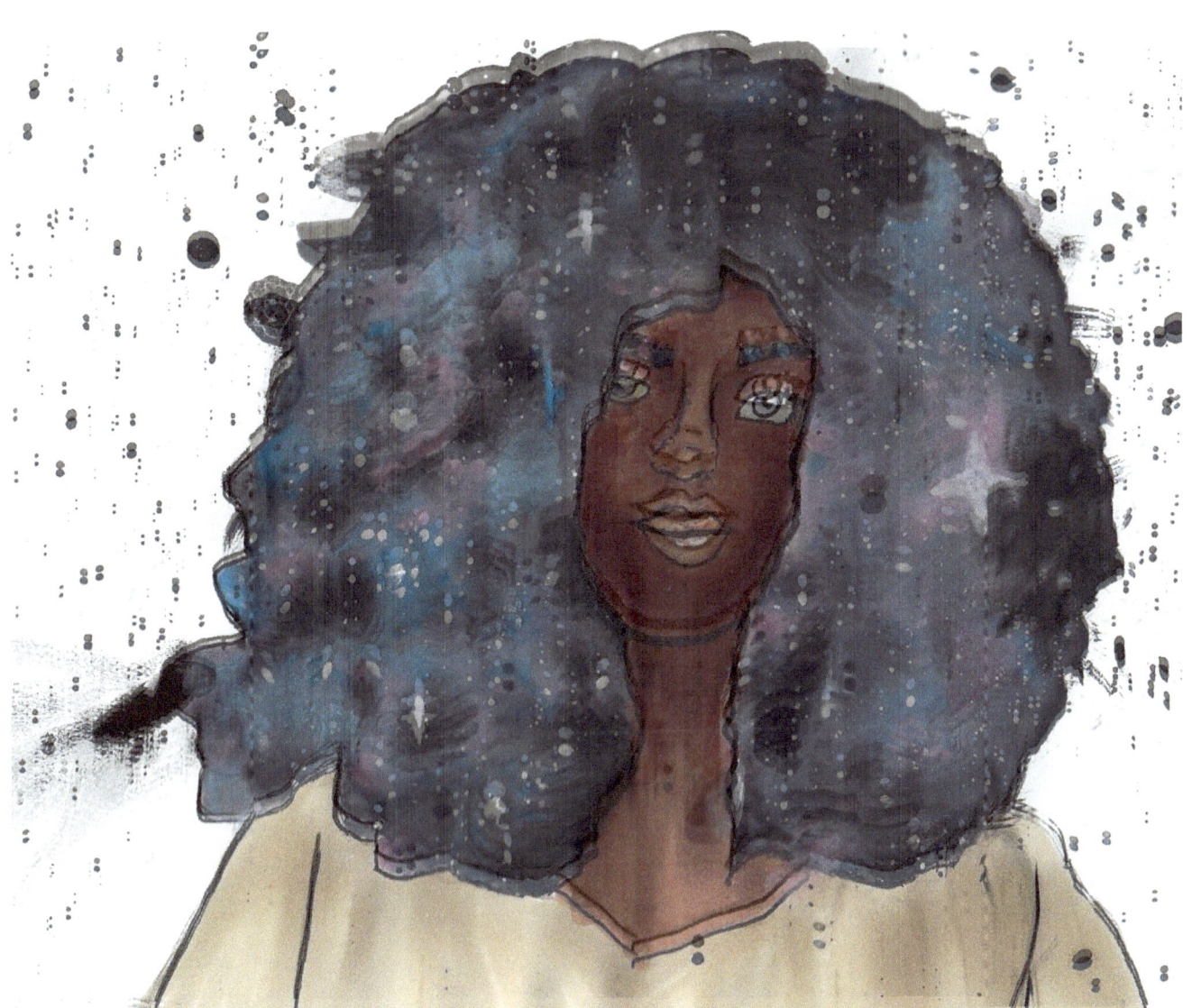

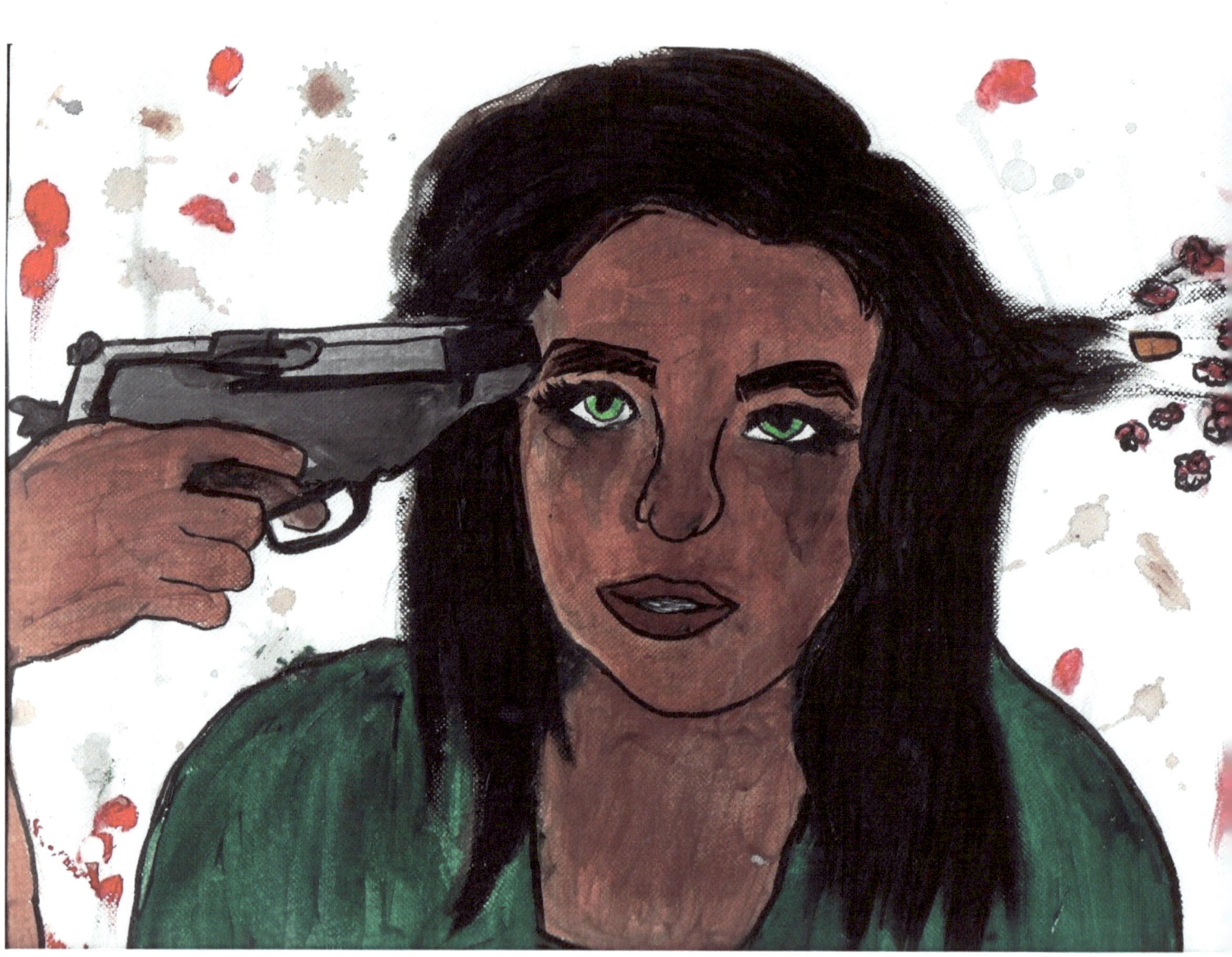

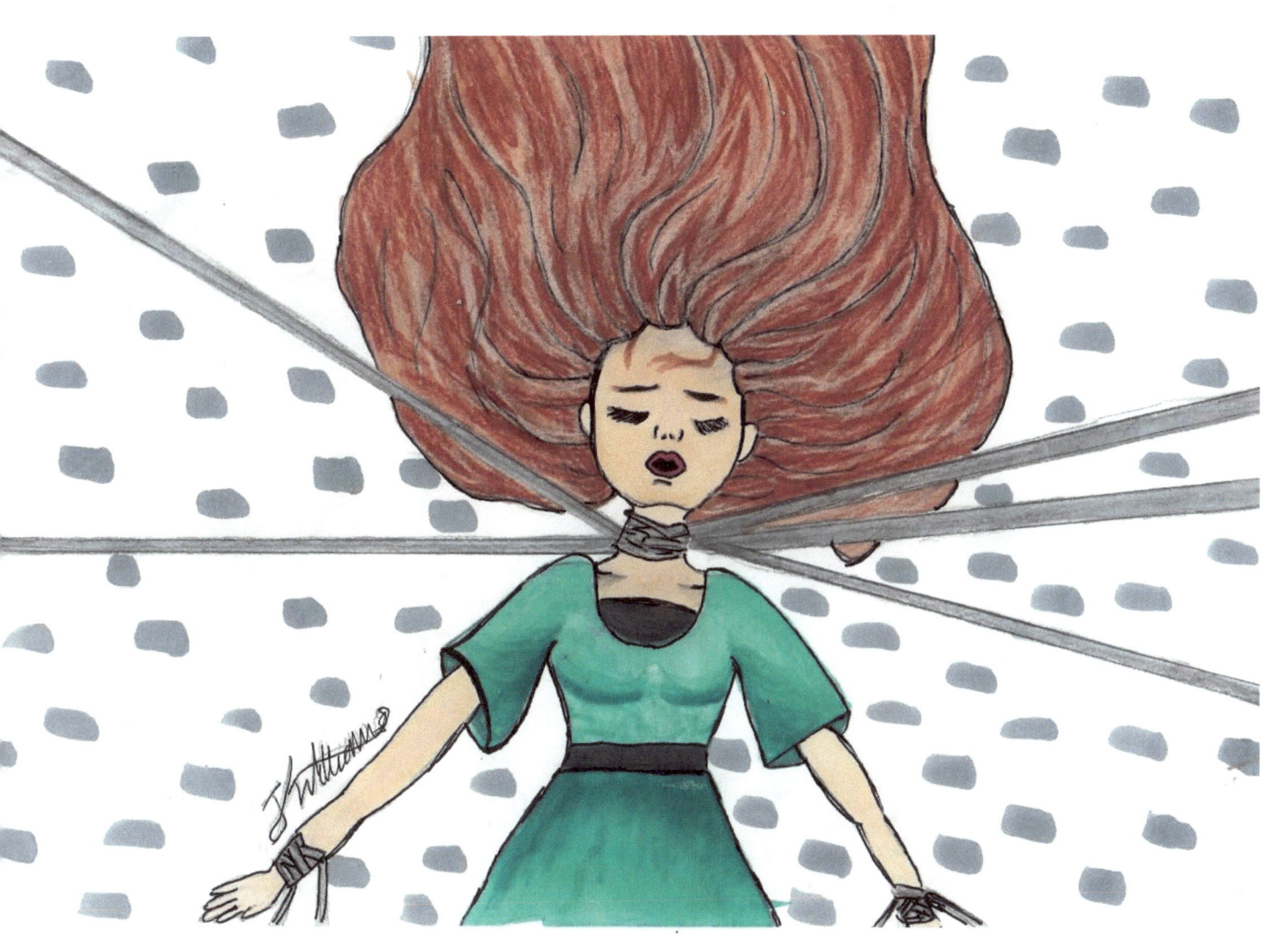

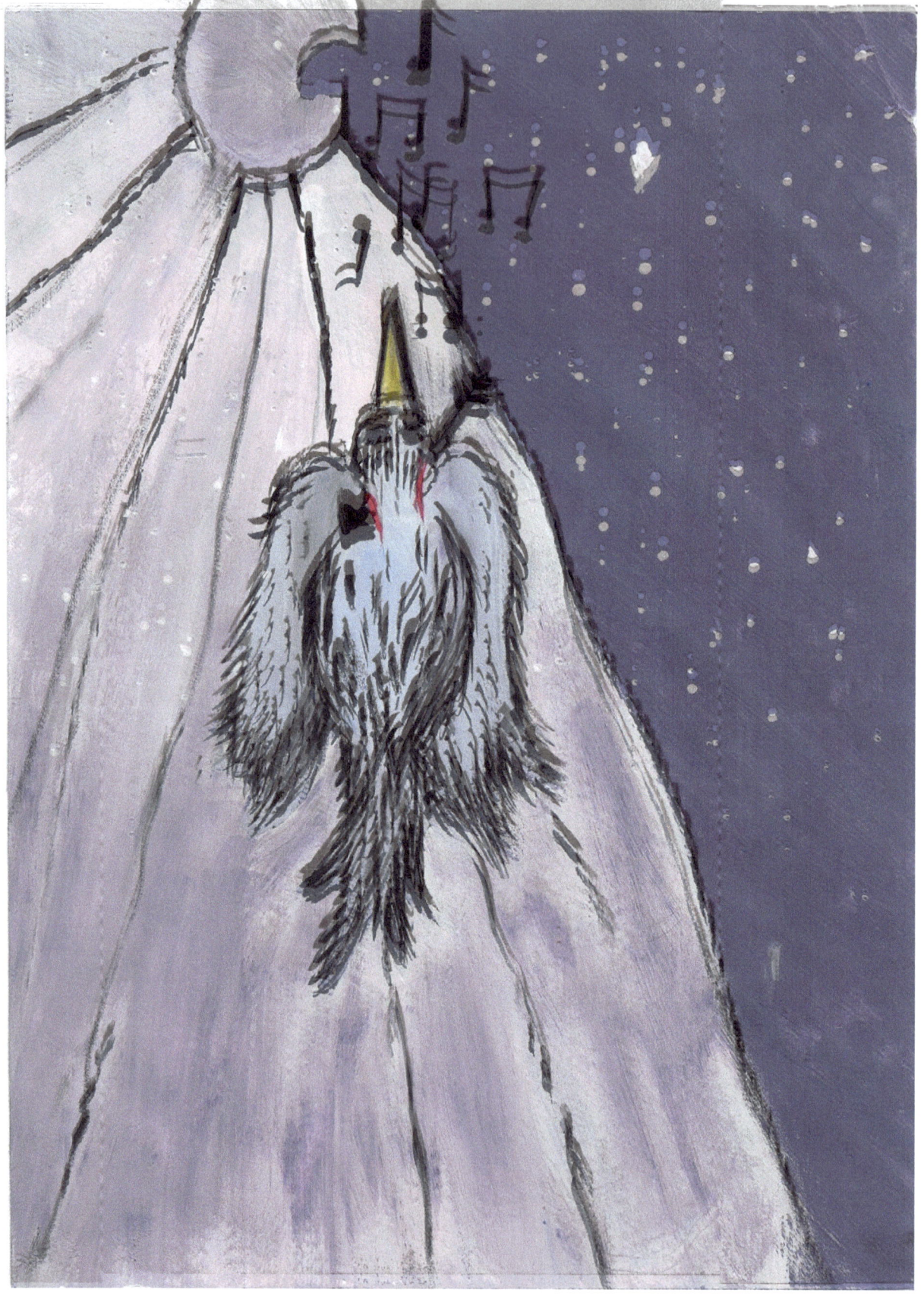

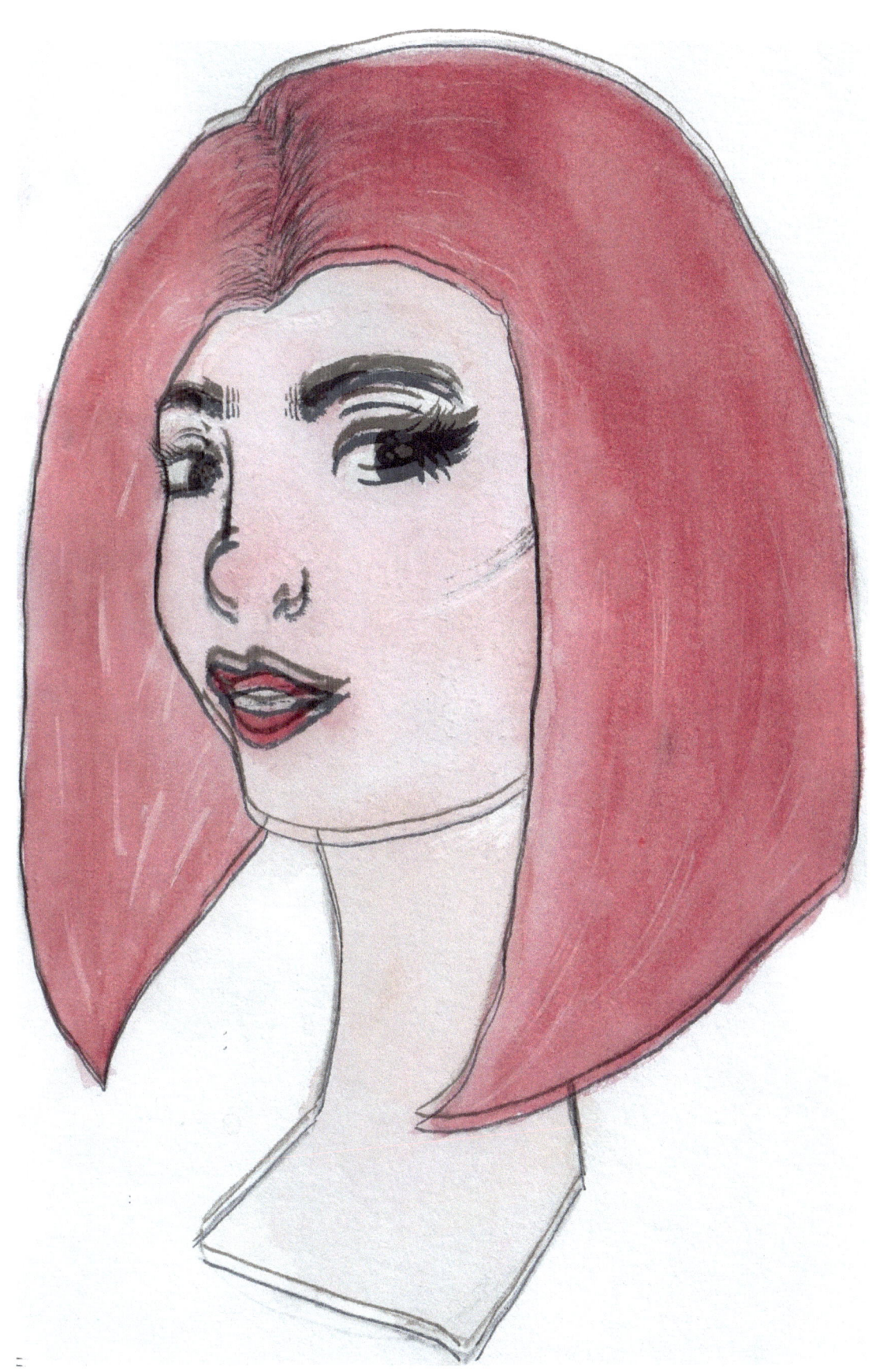

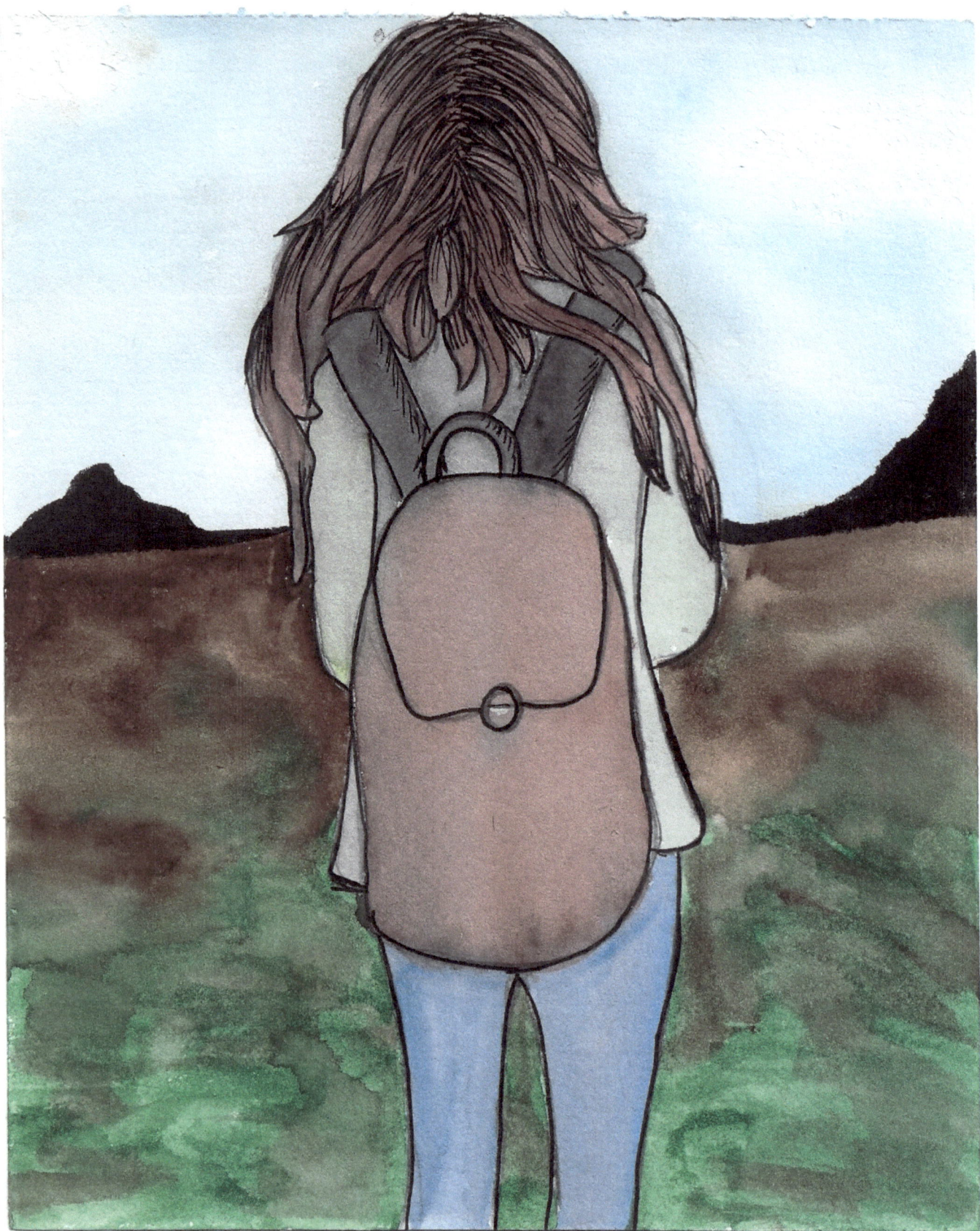

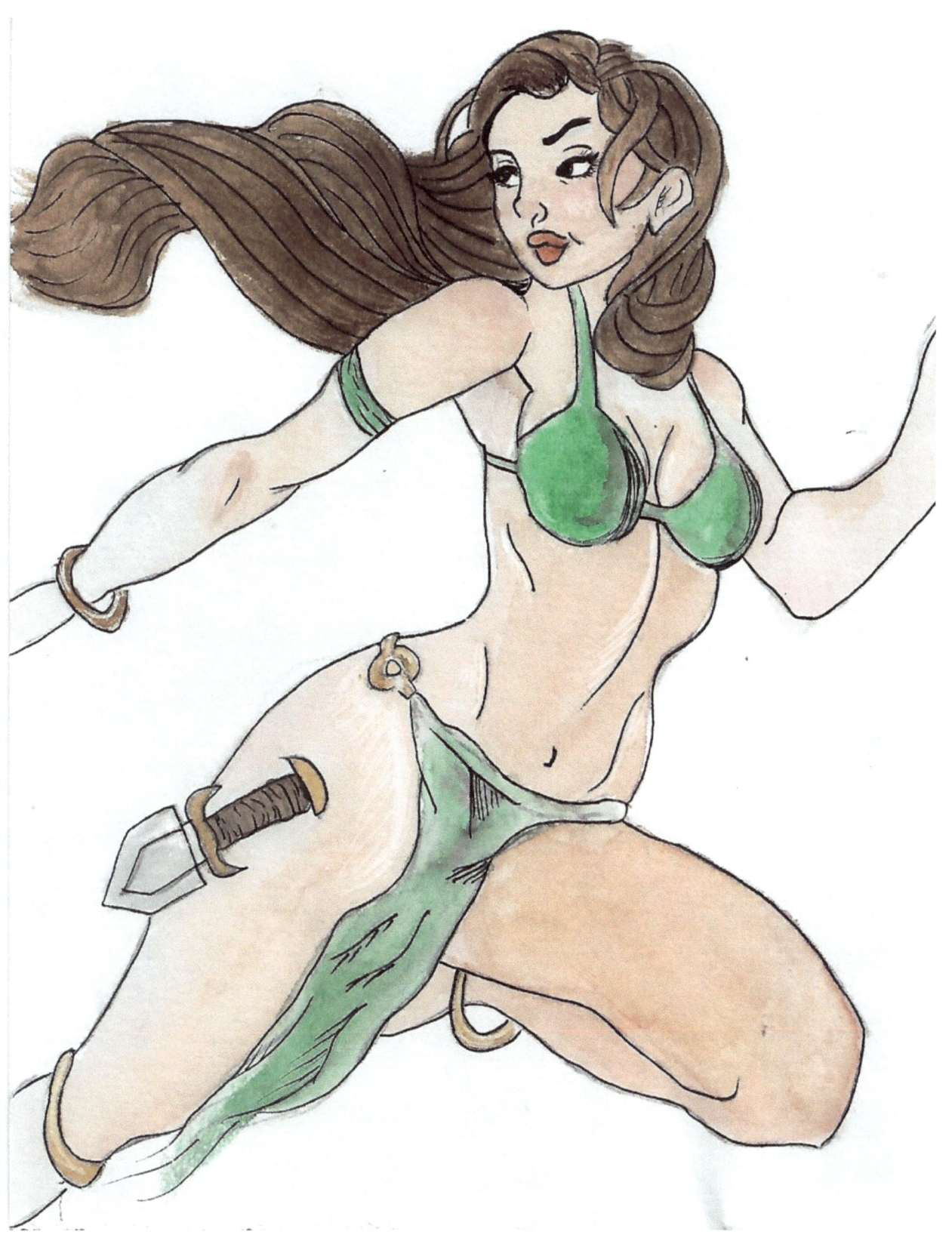

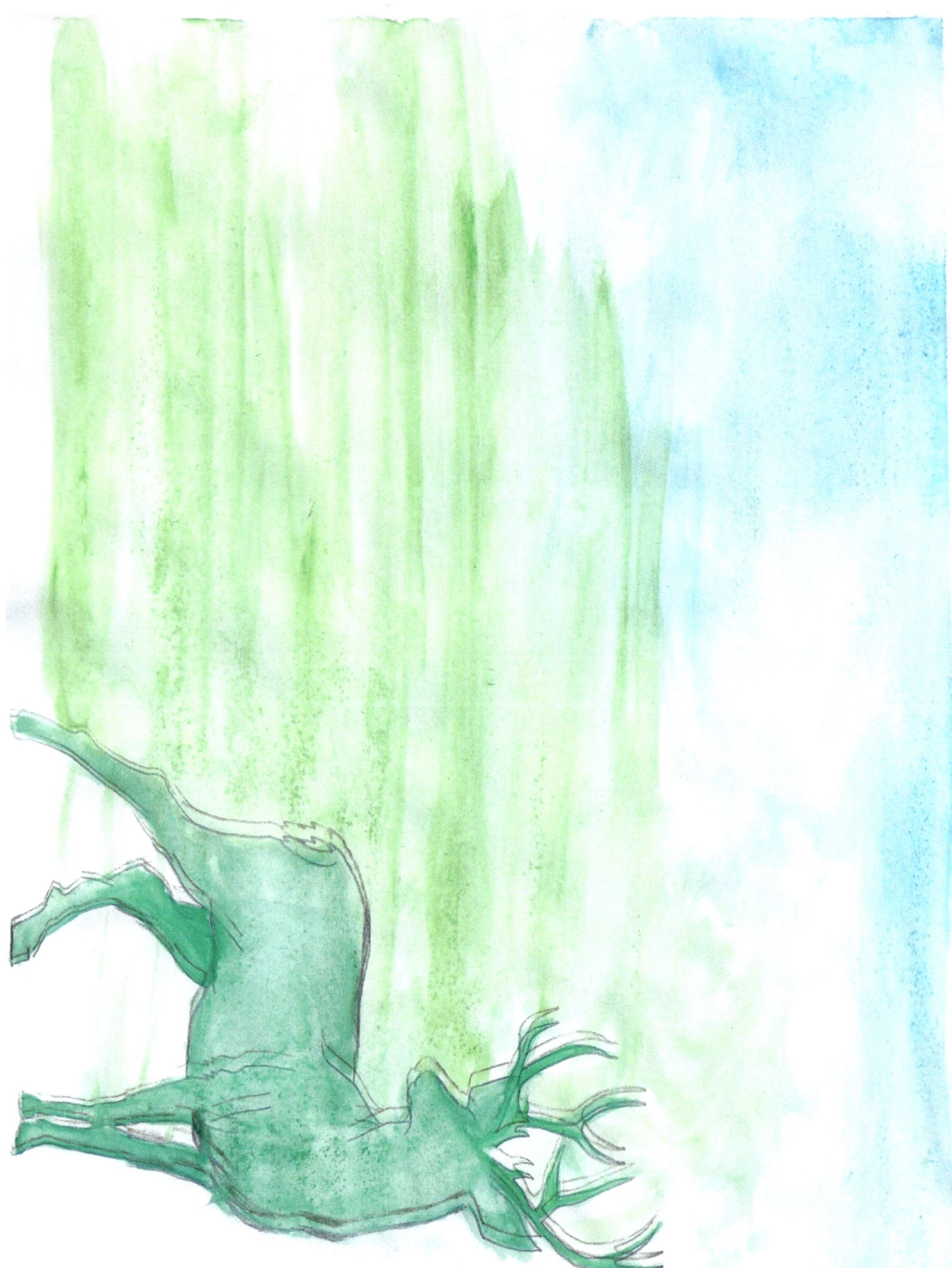

2016

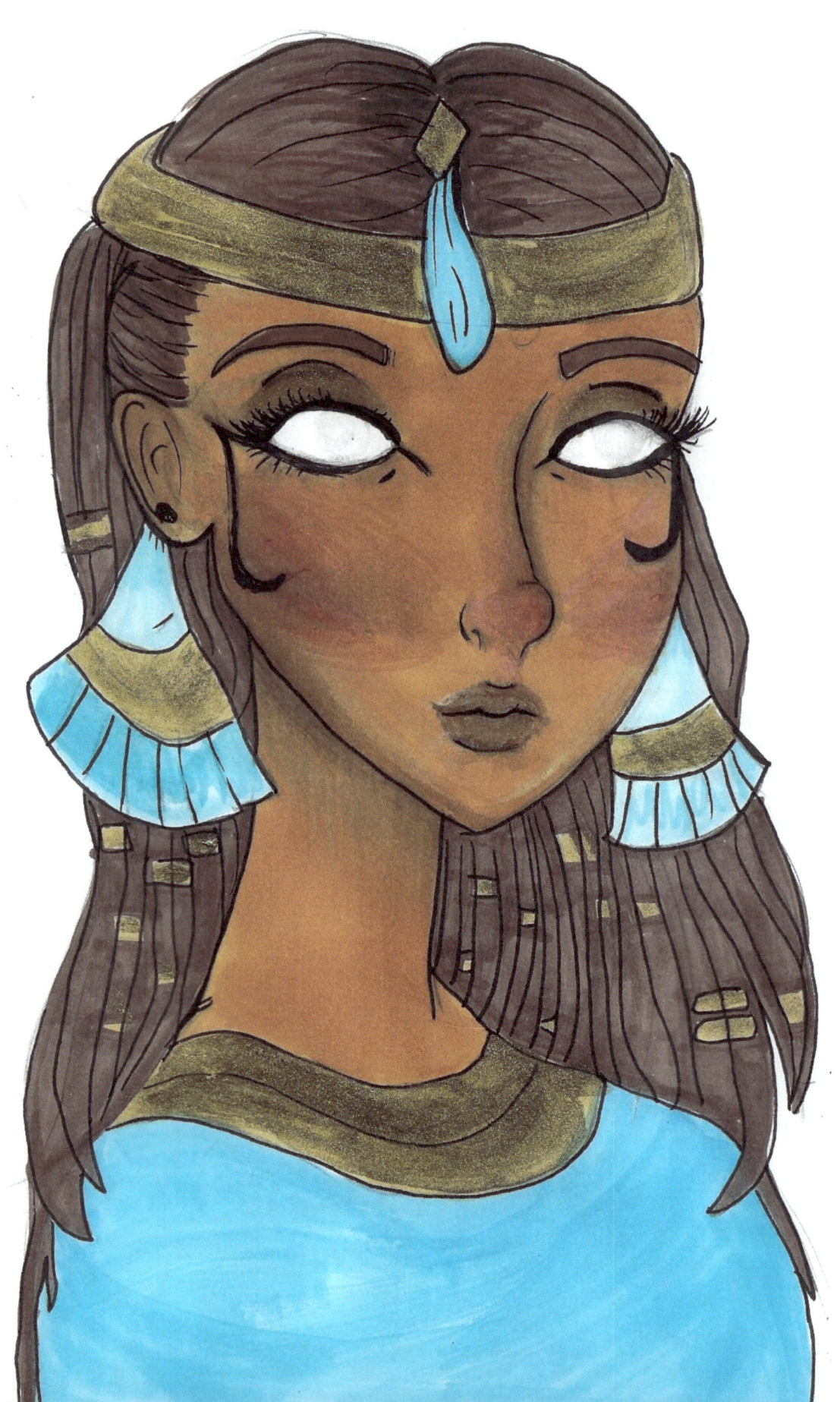

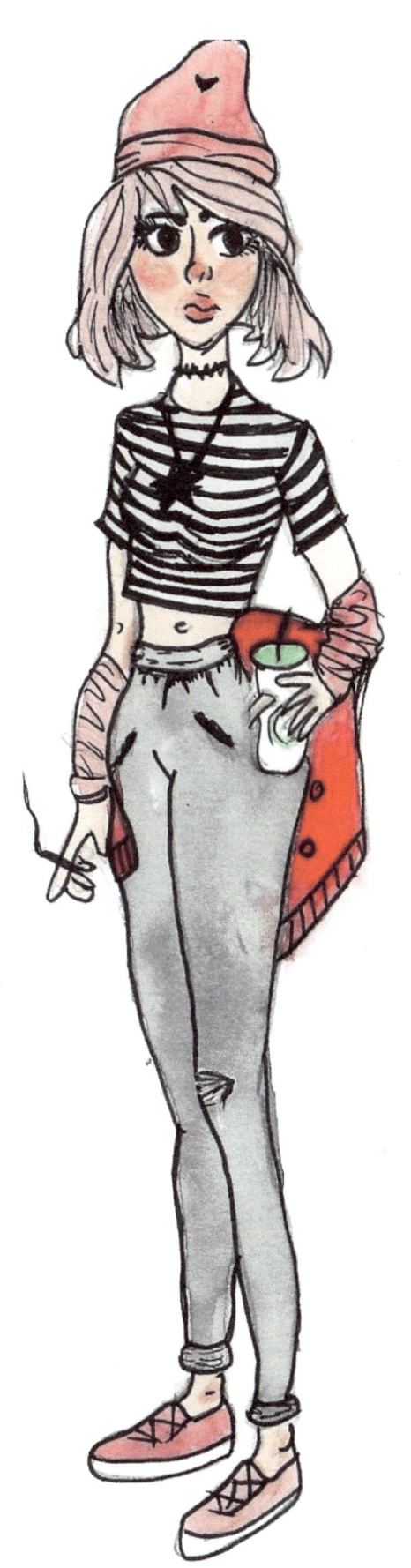

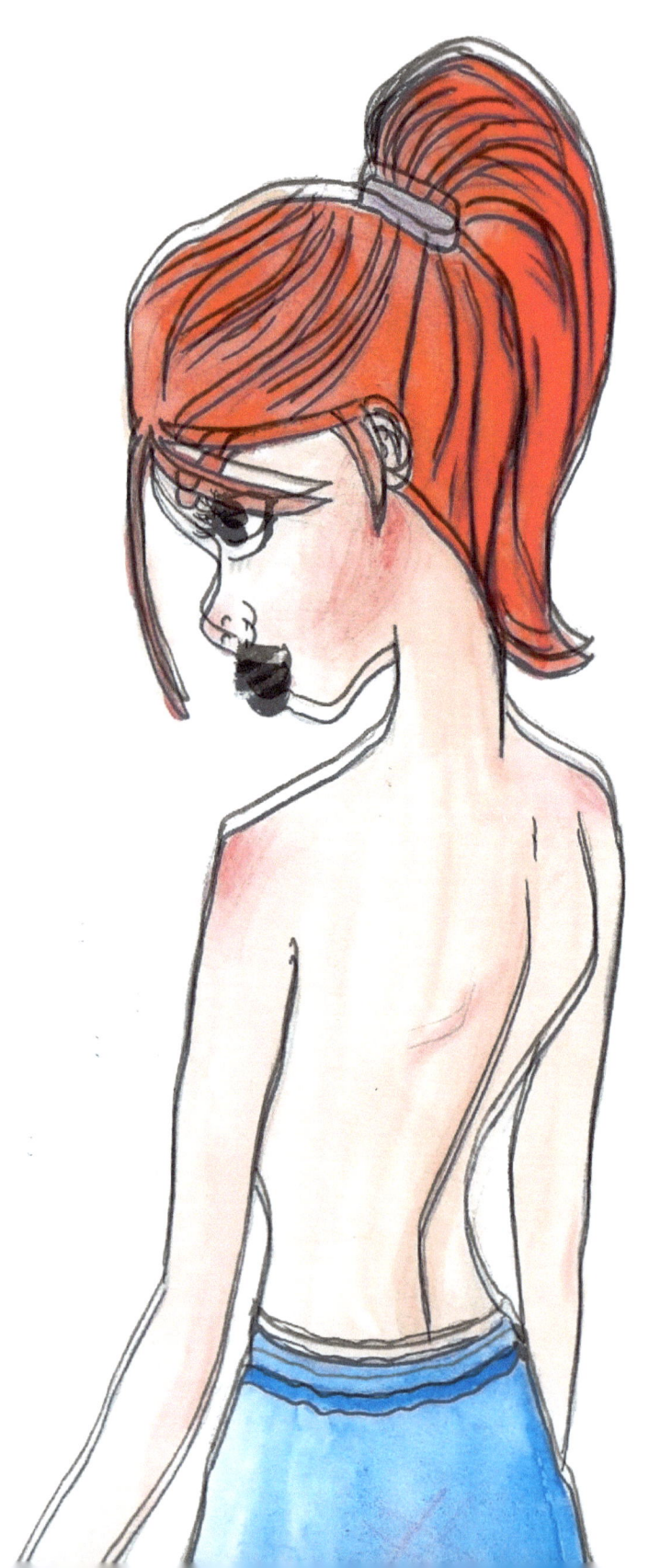

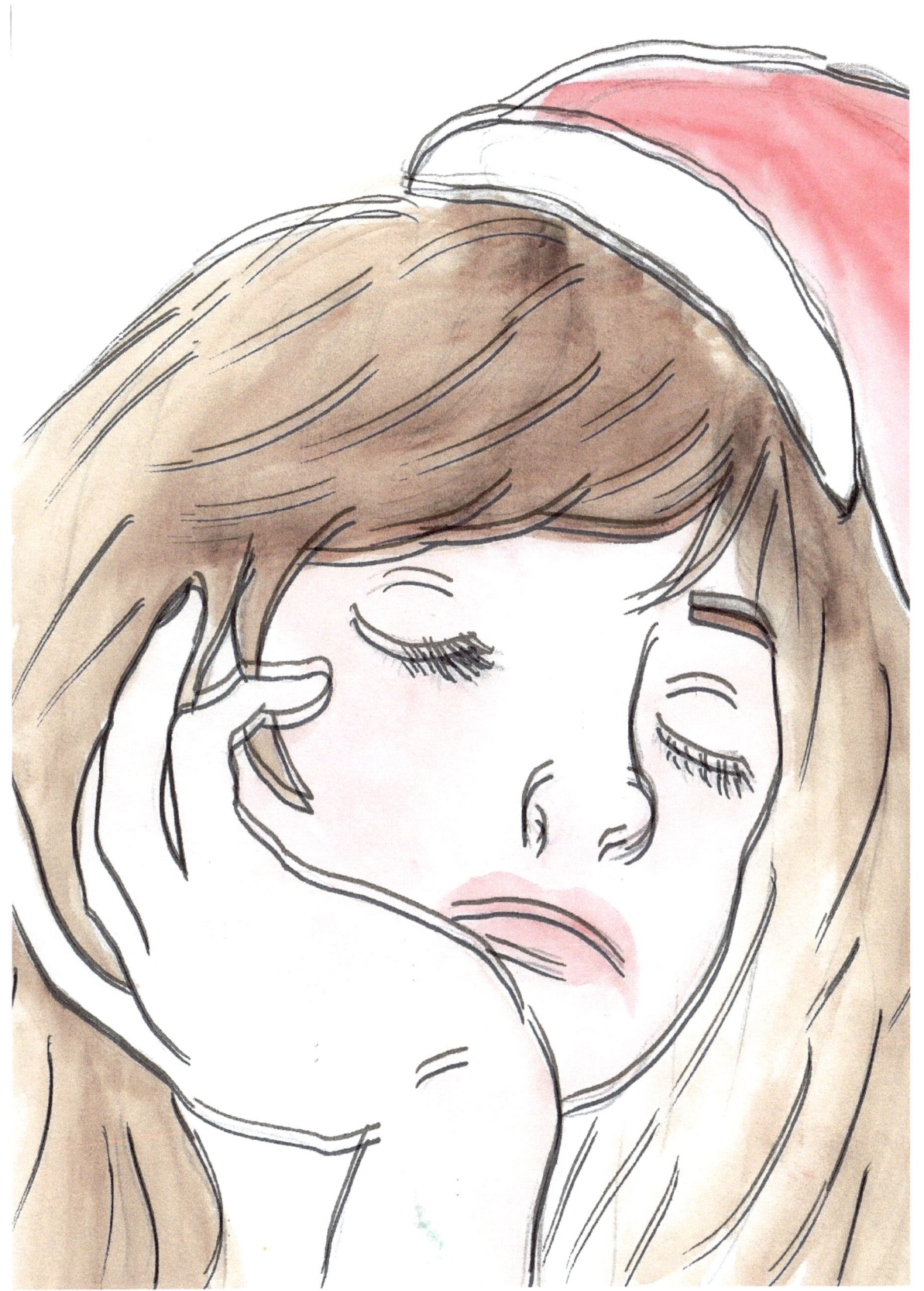

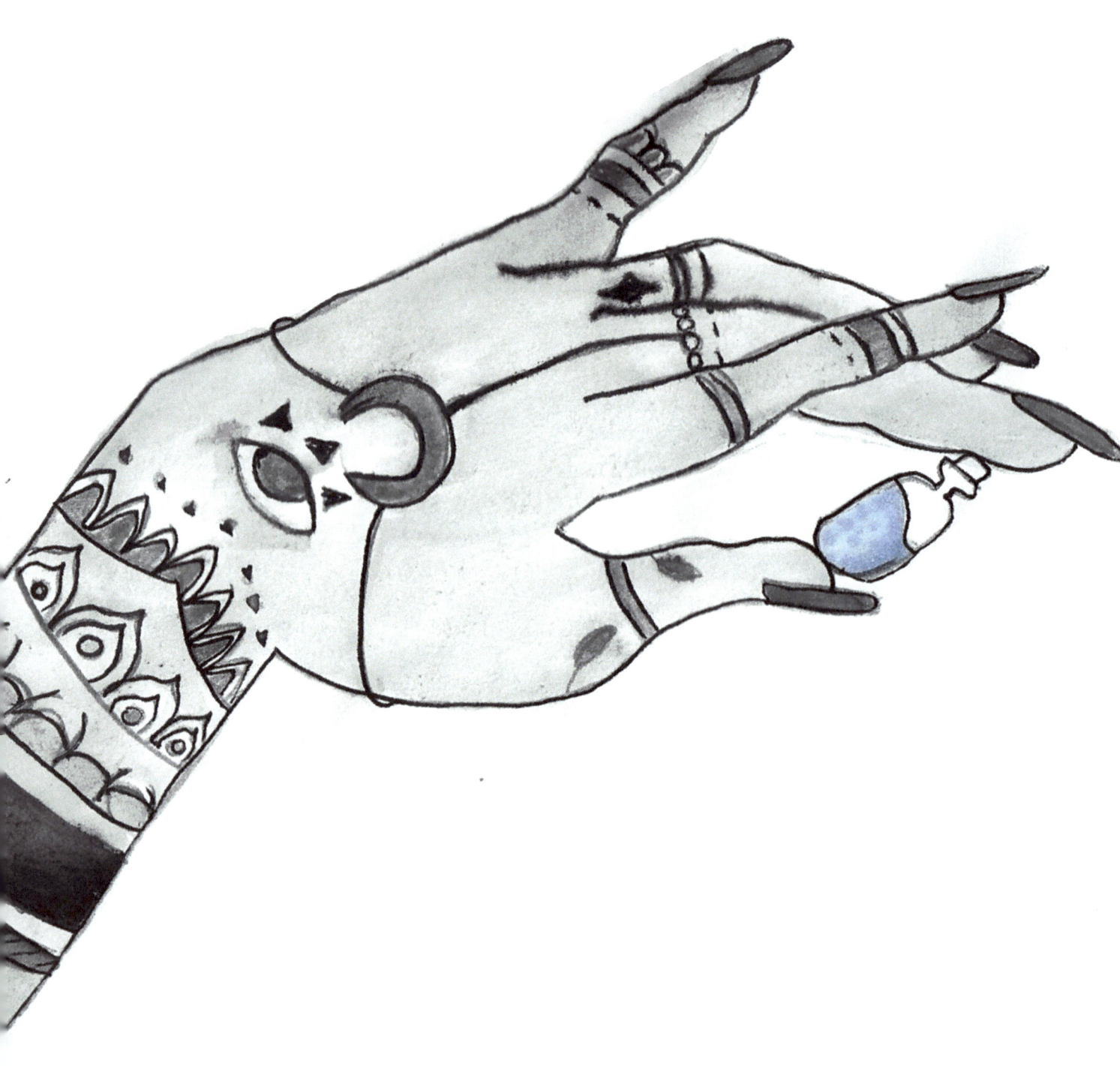

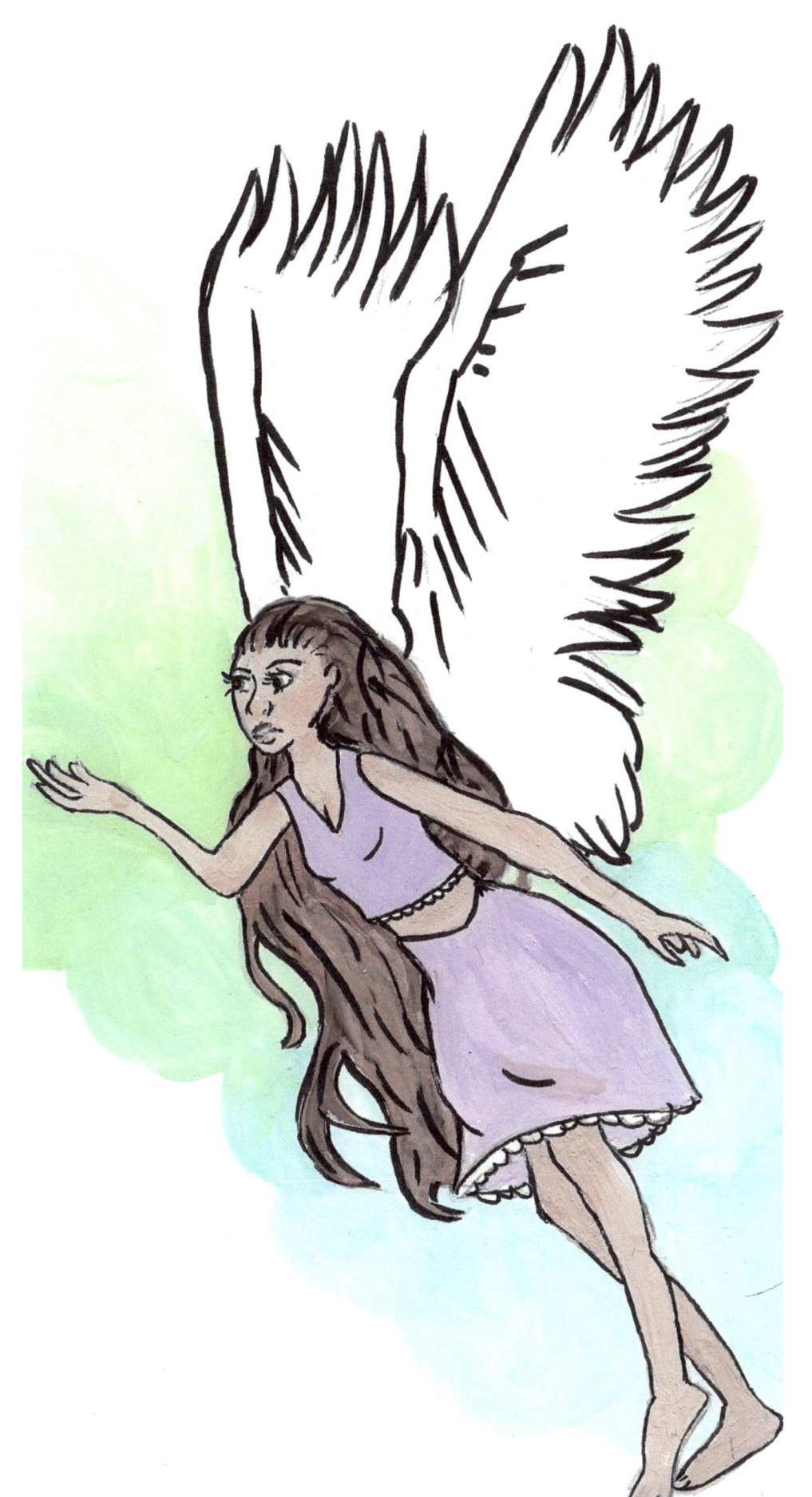

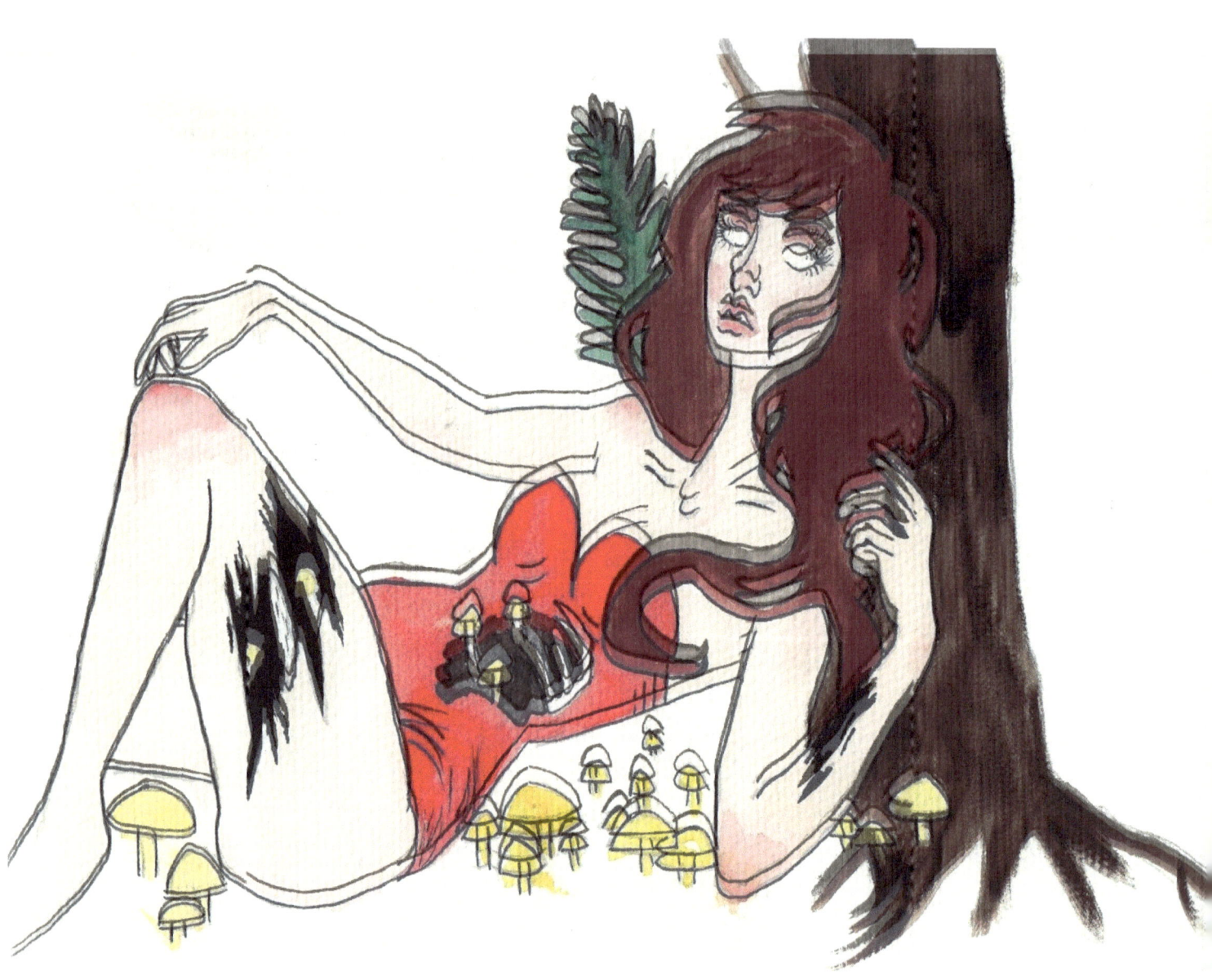

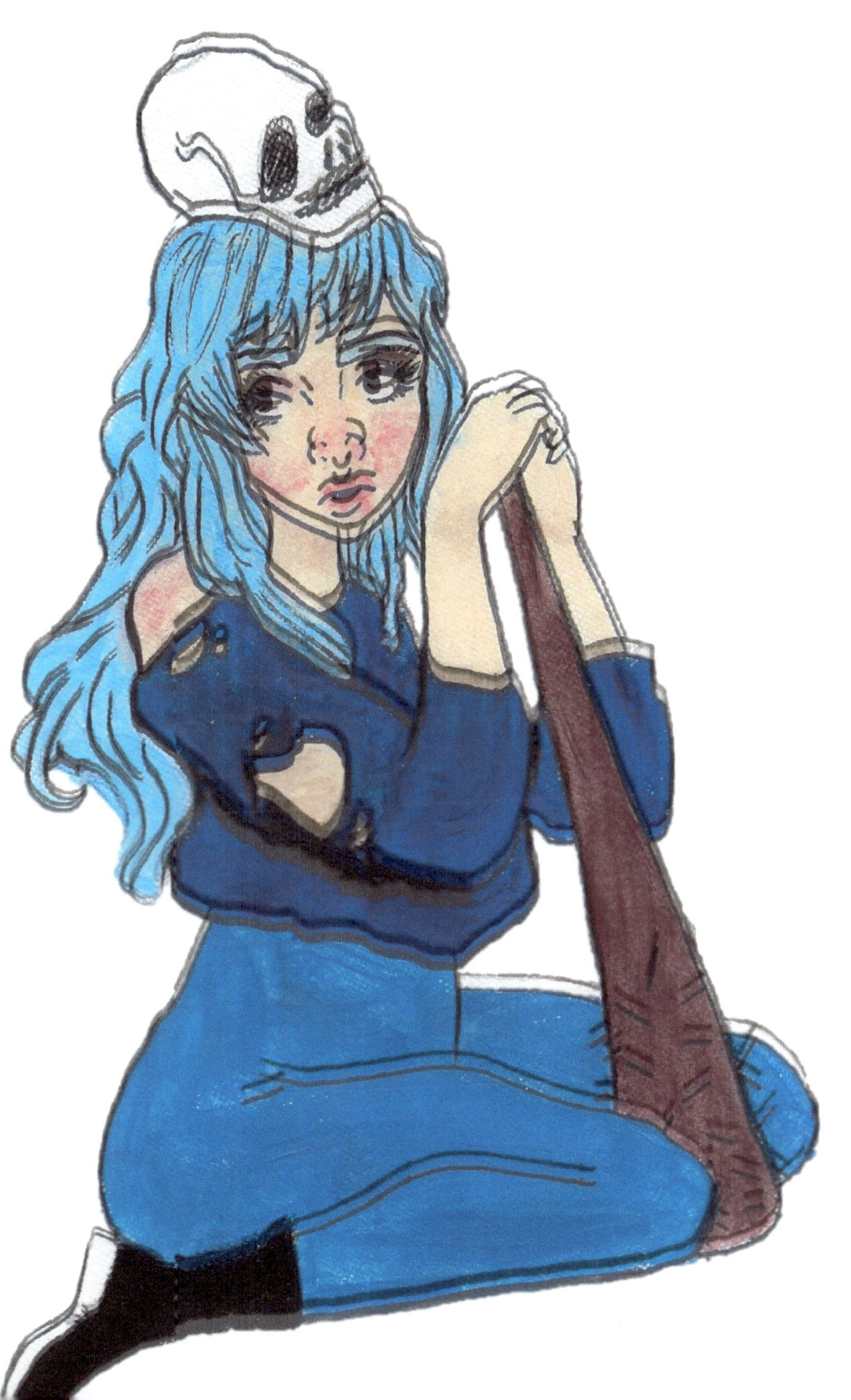

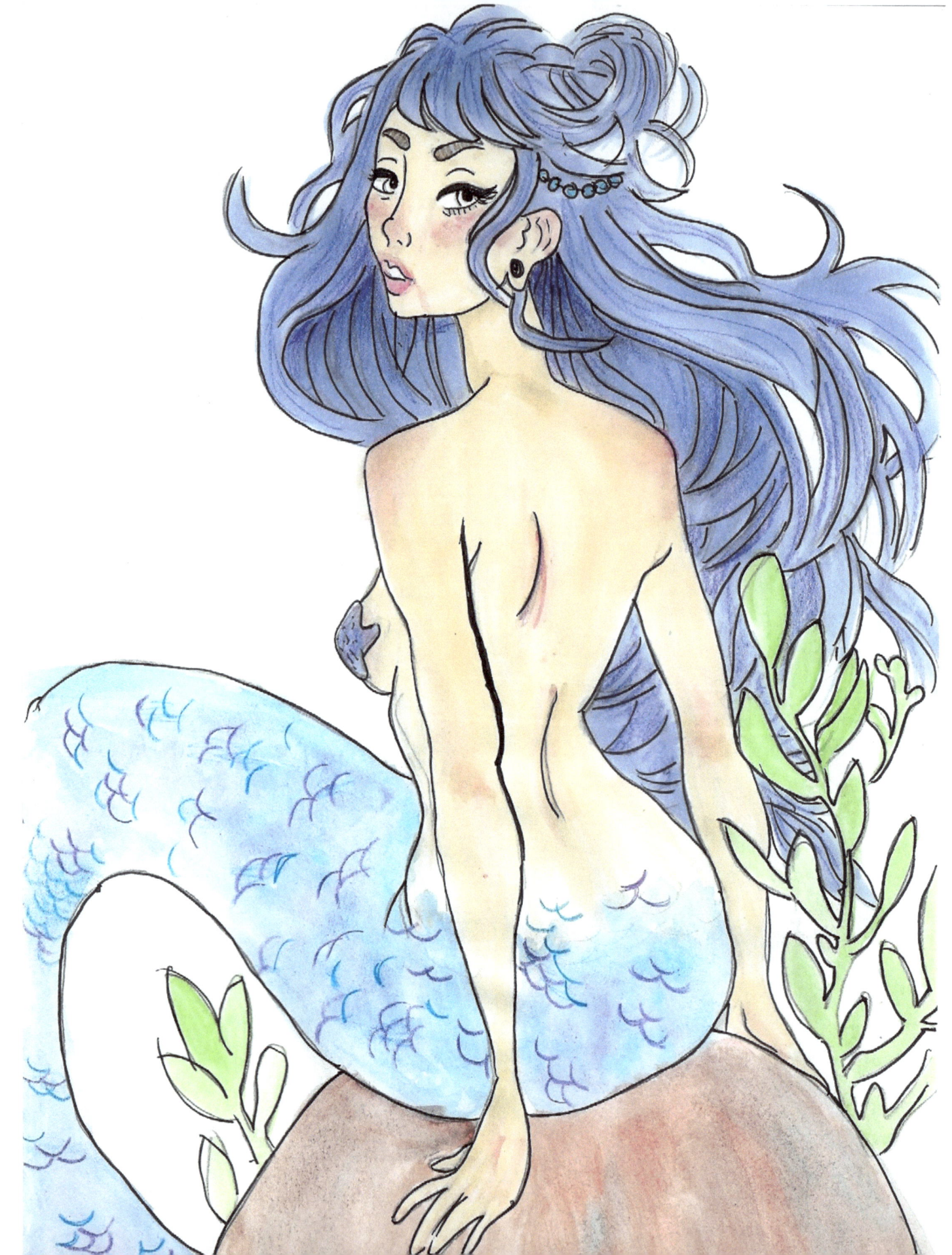

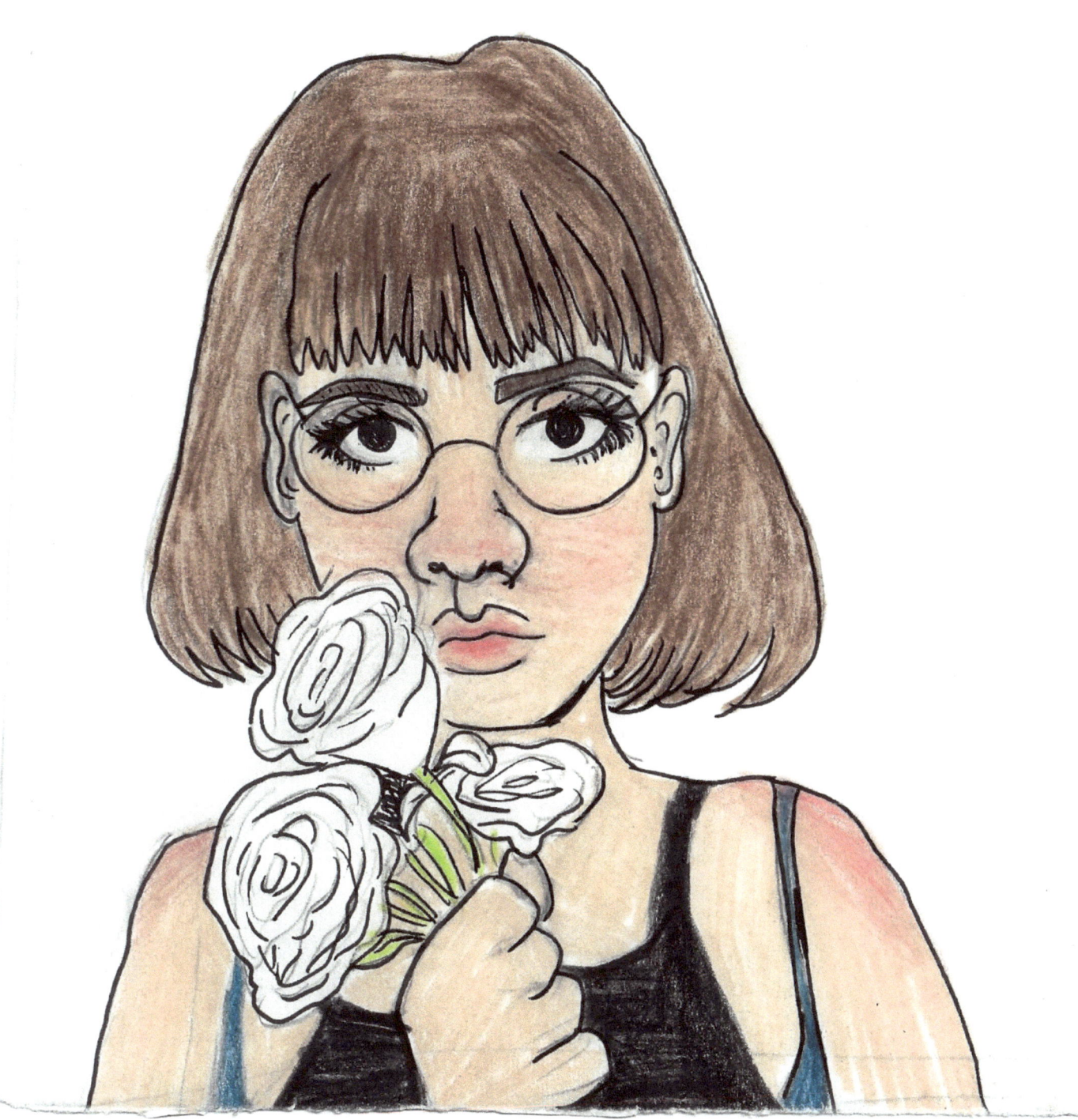

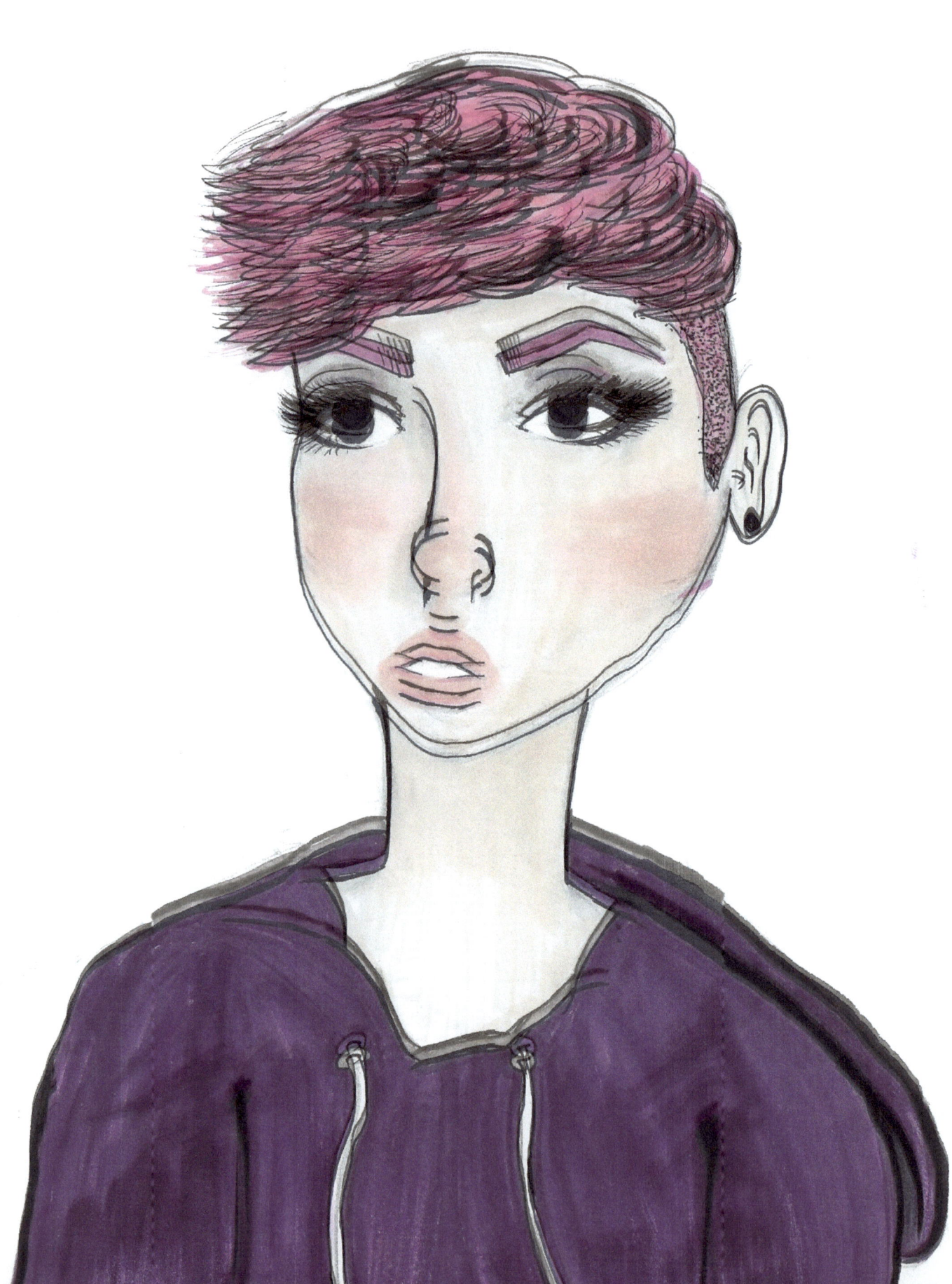

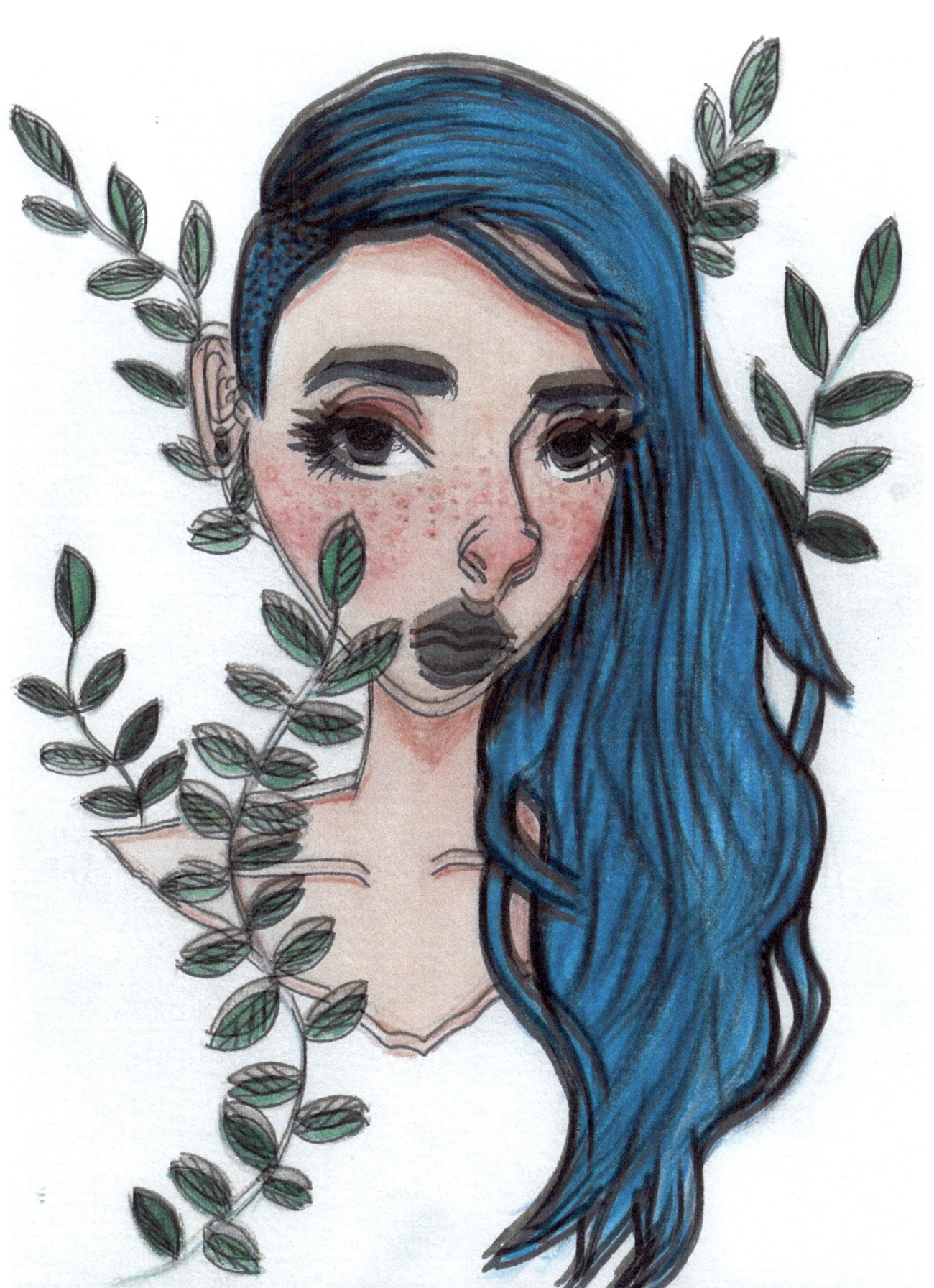

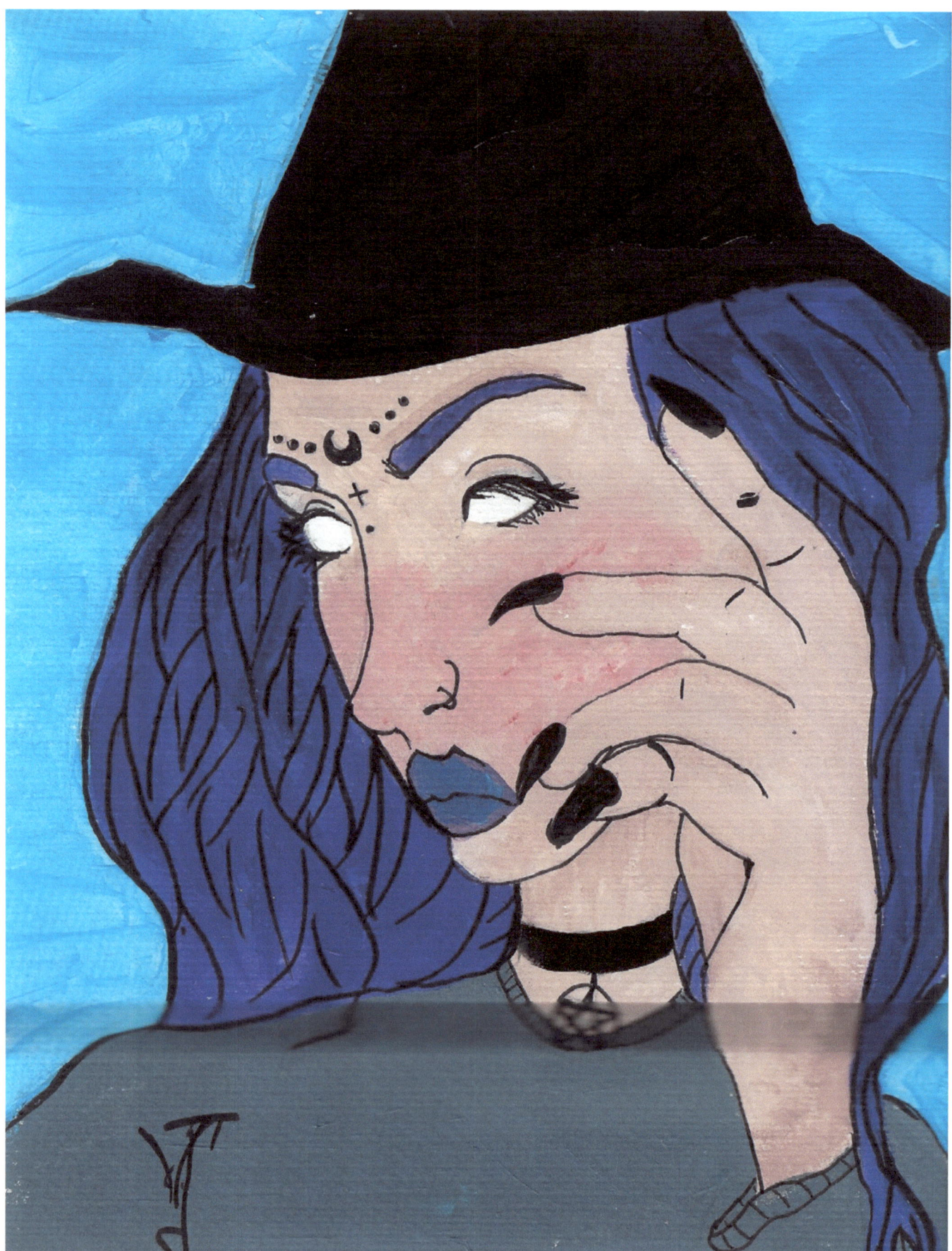

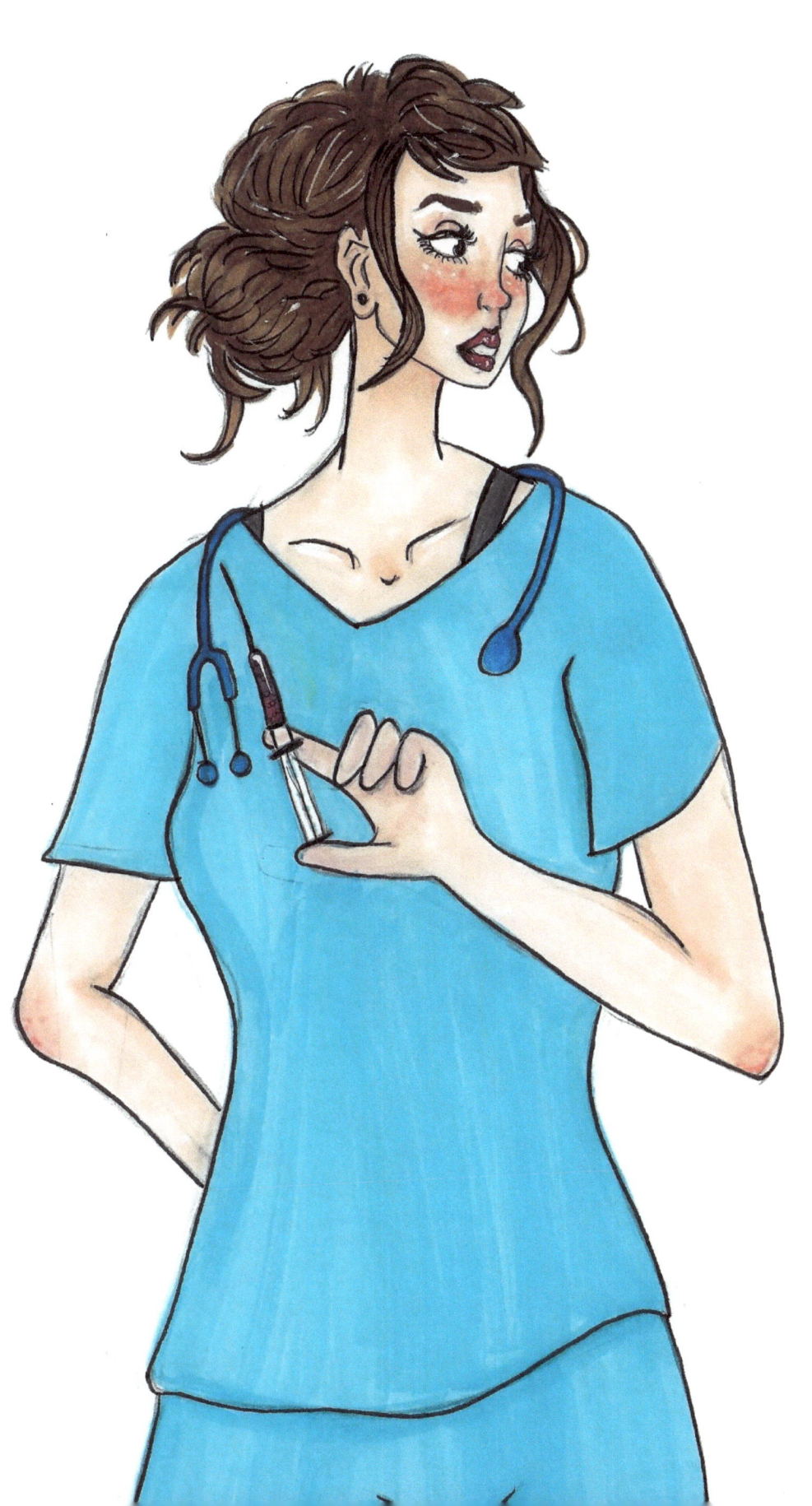

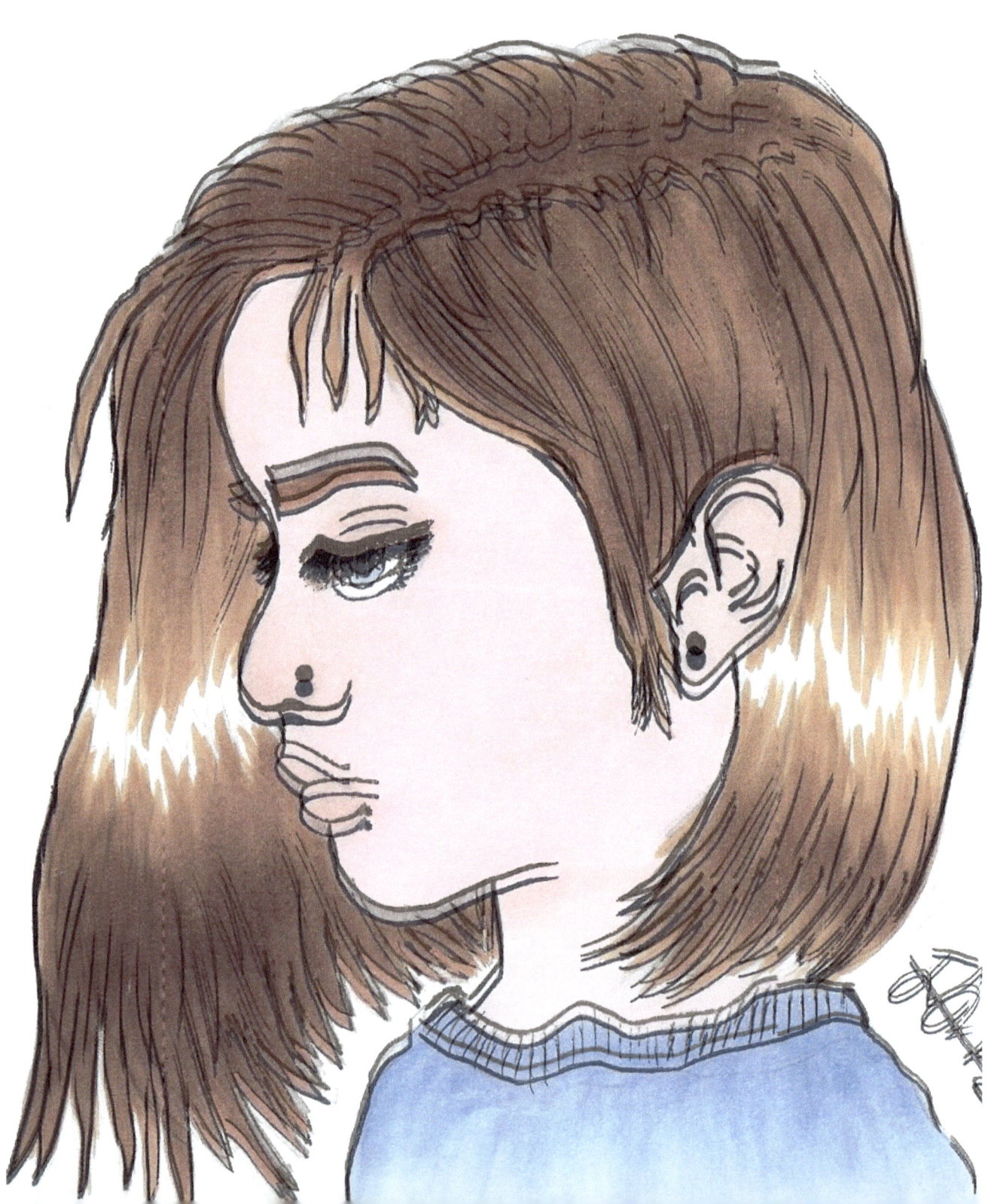

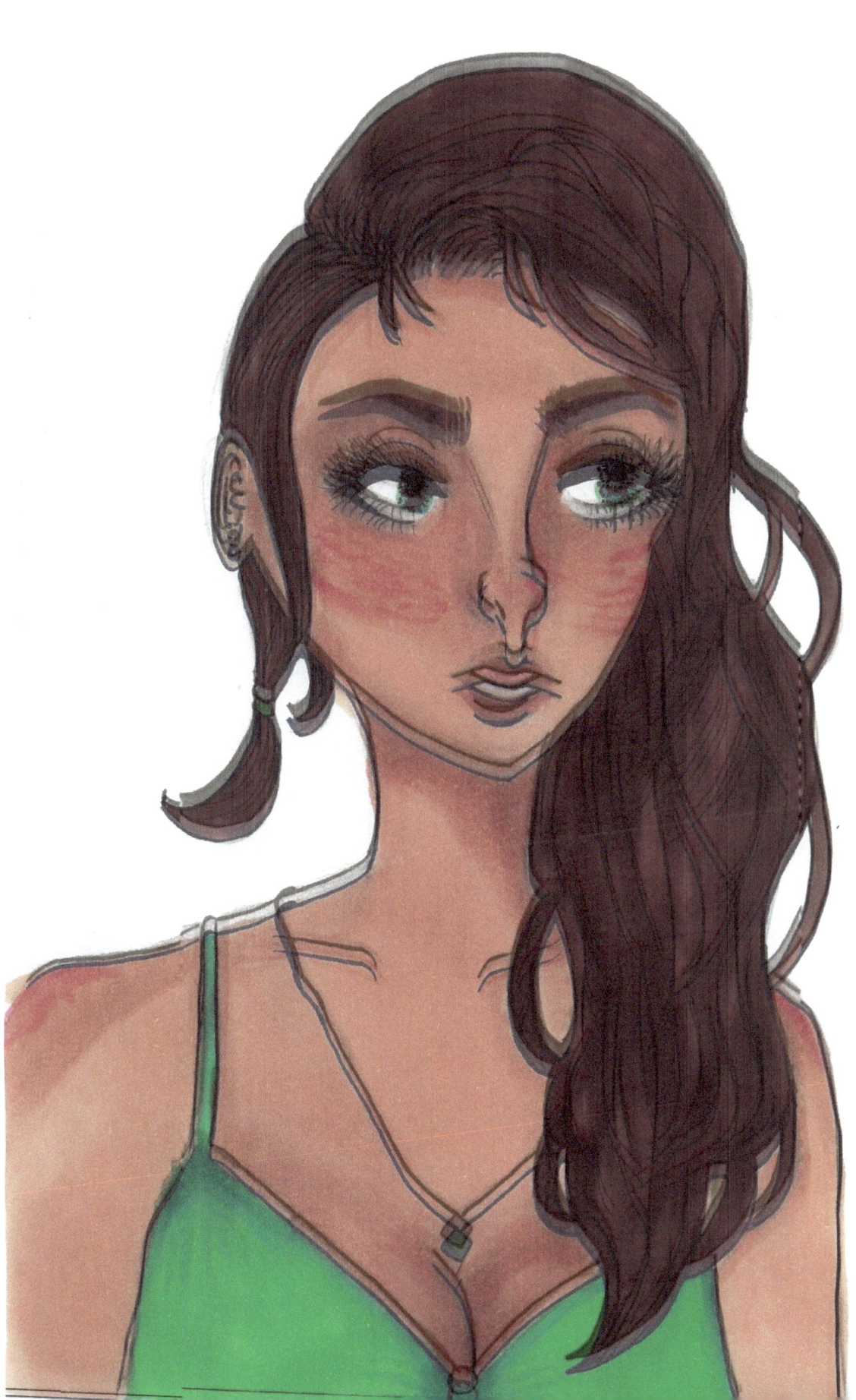

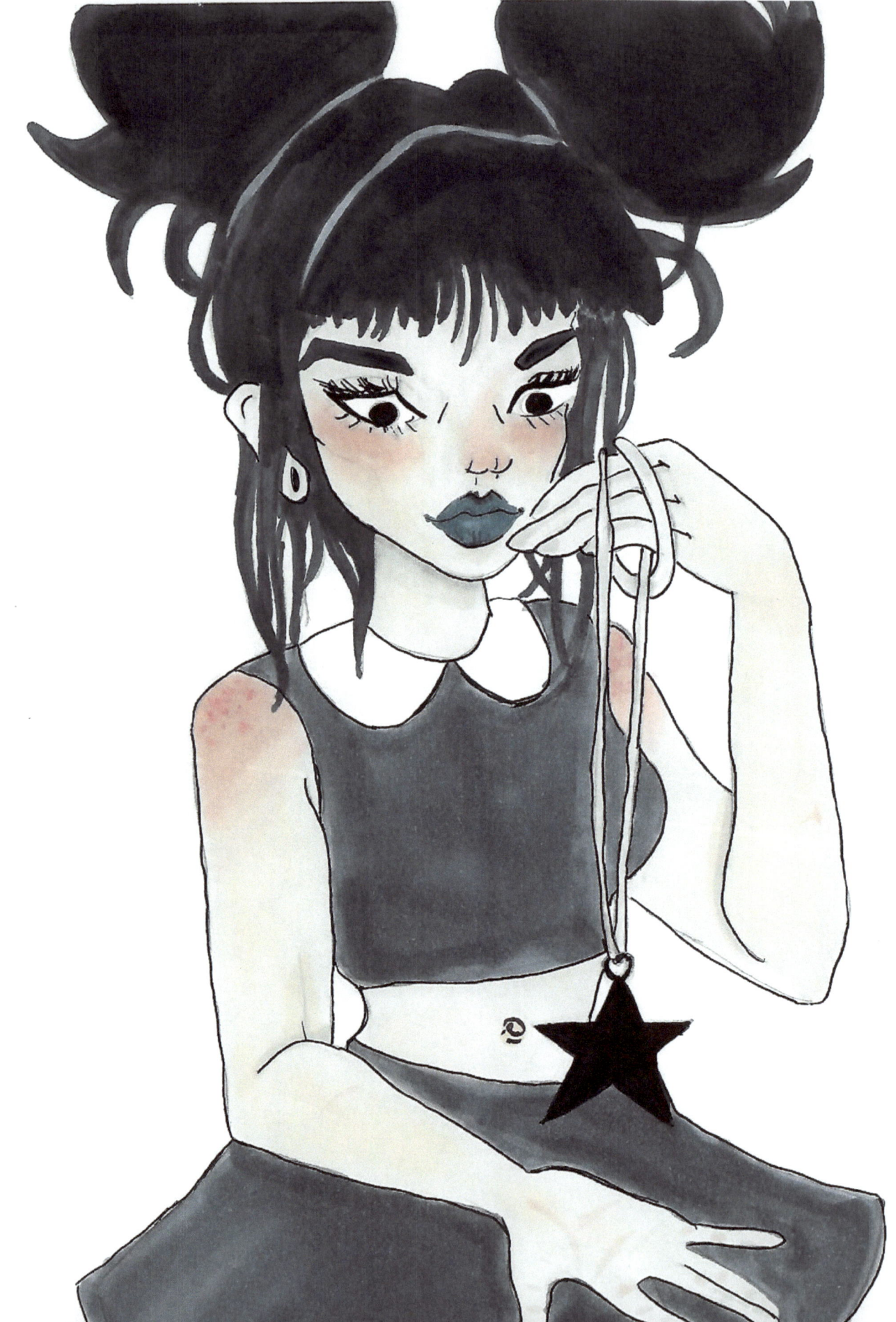

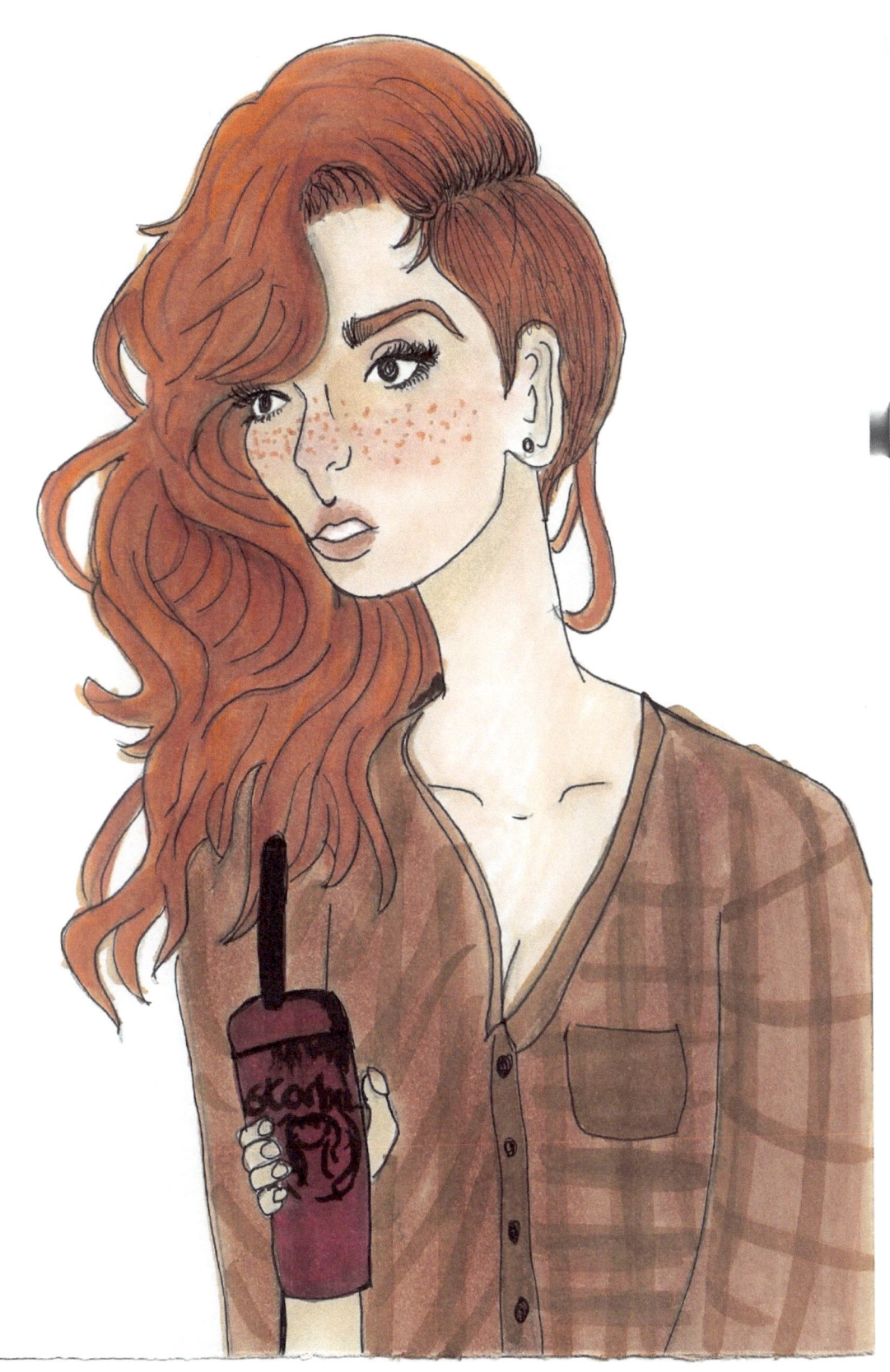

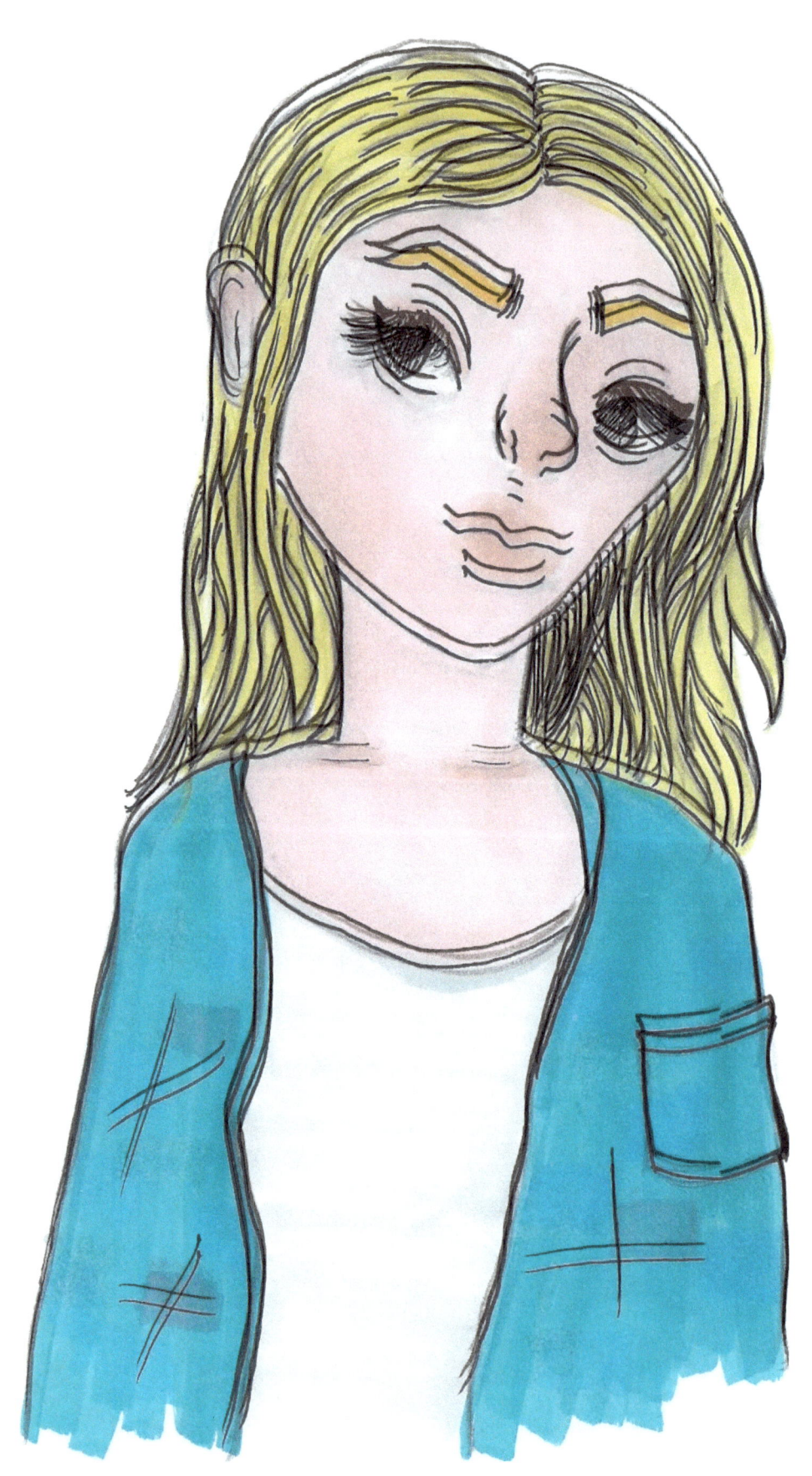

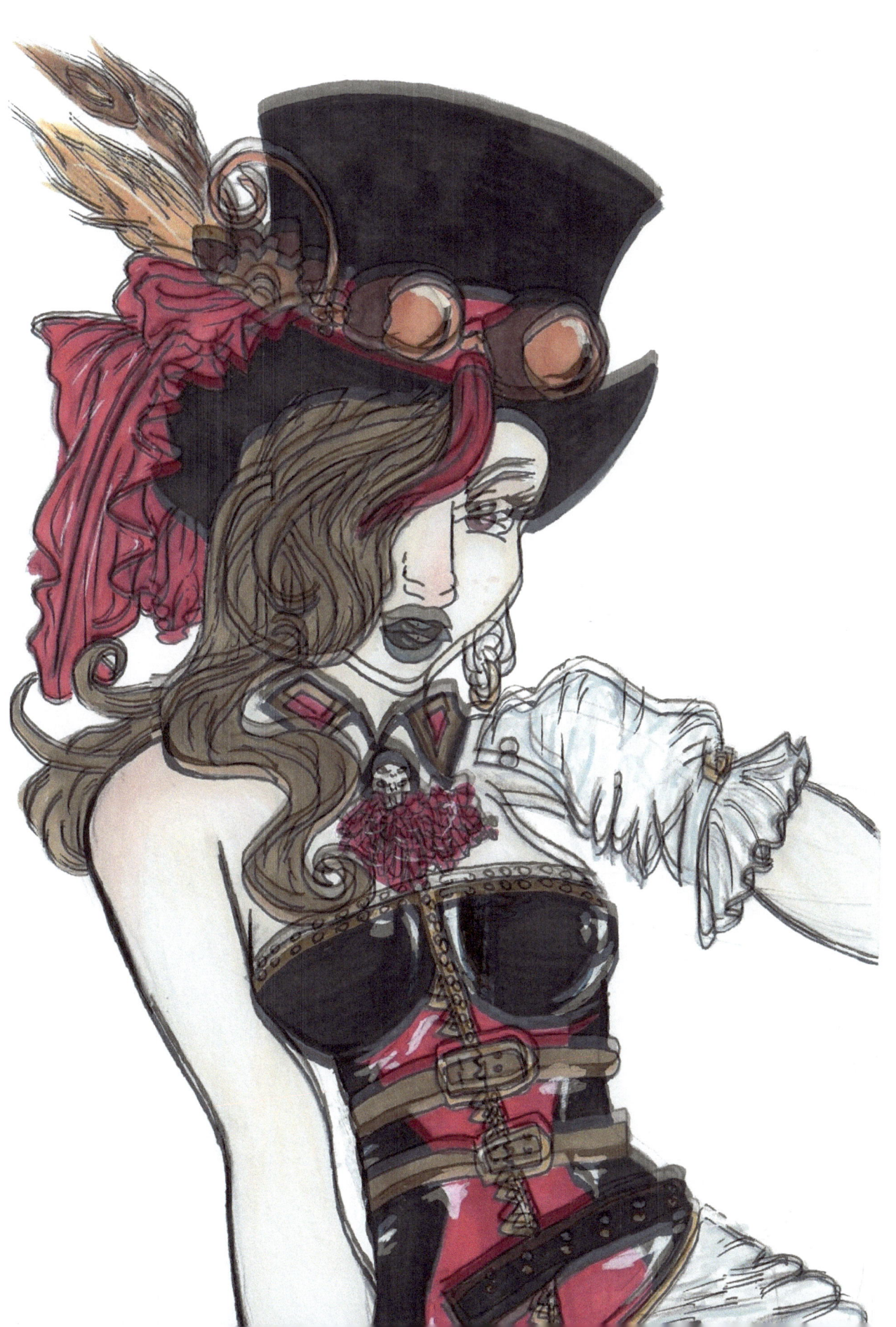

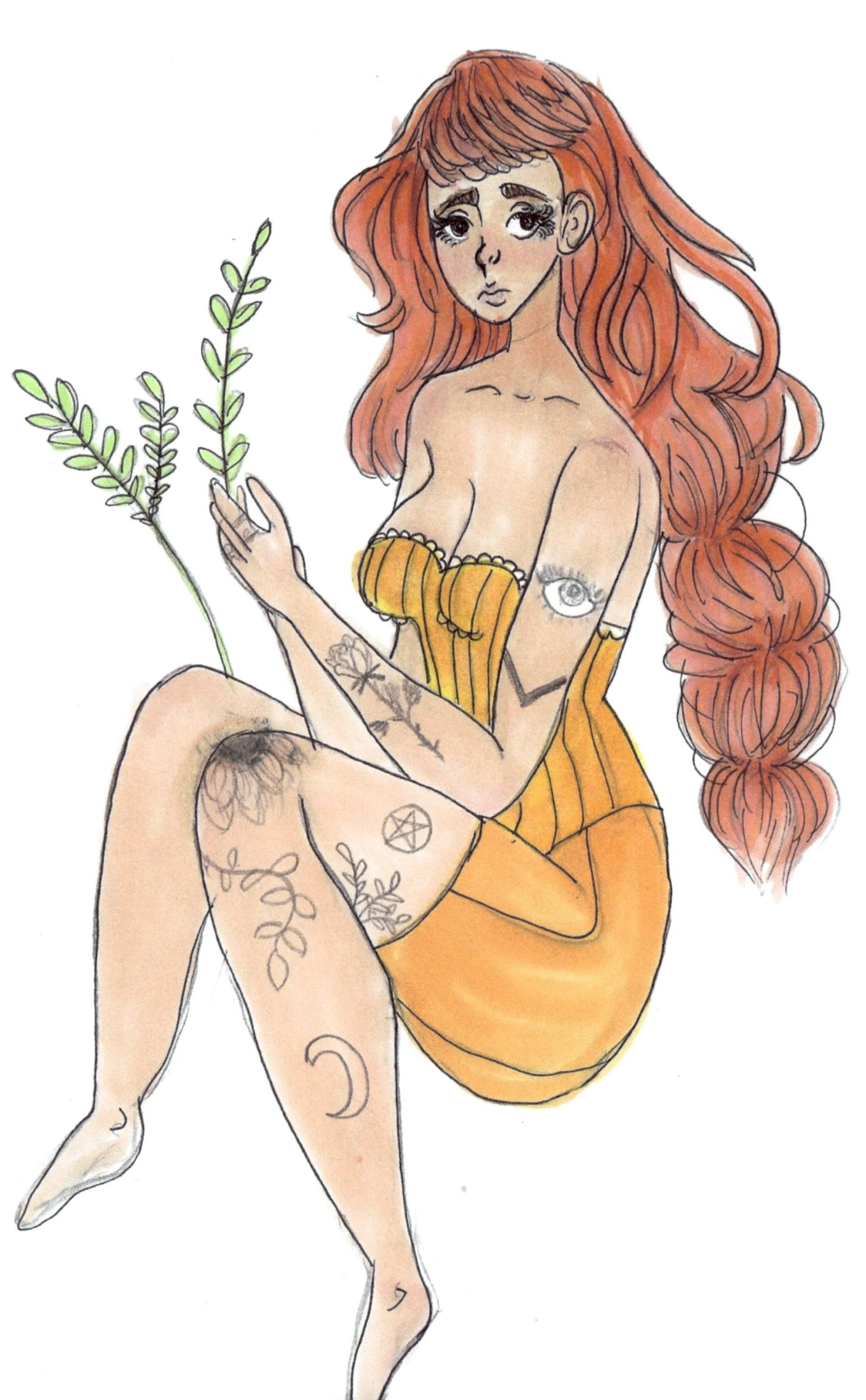

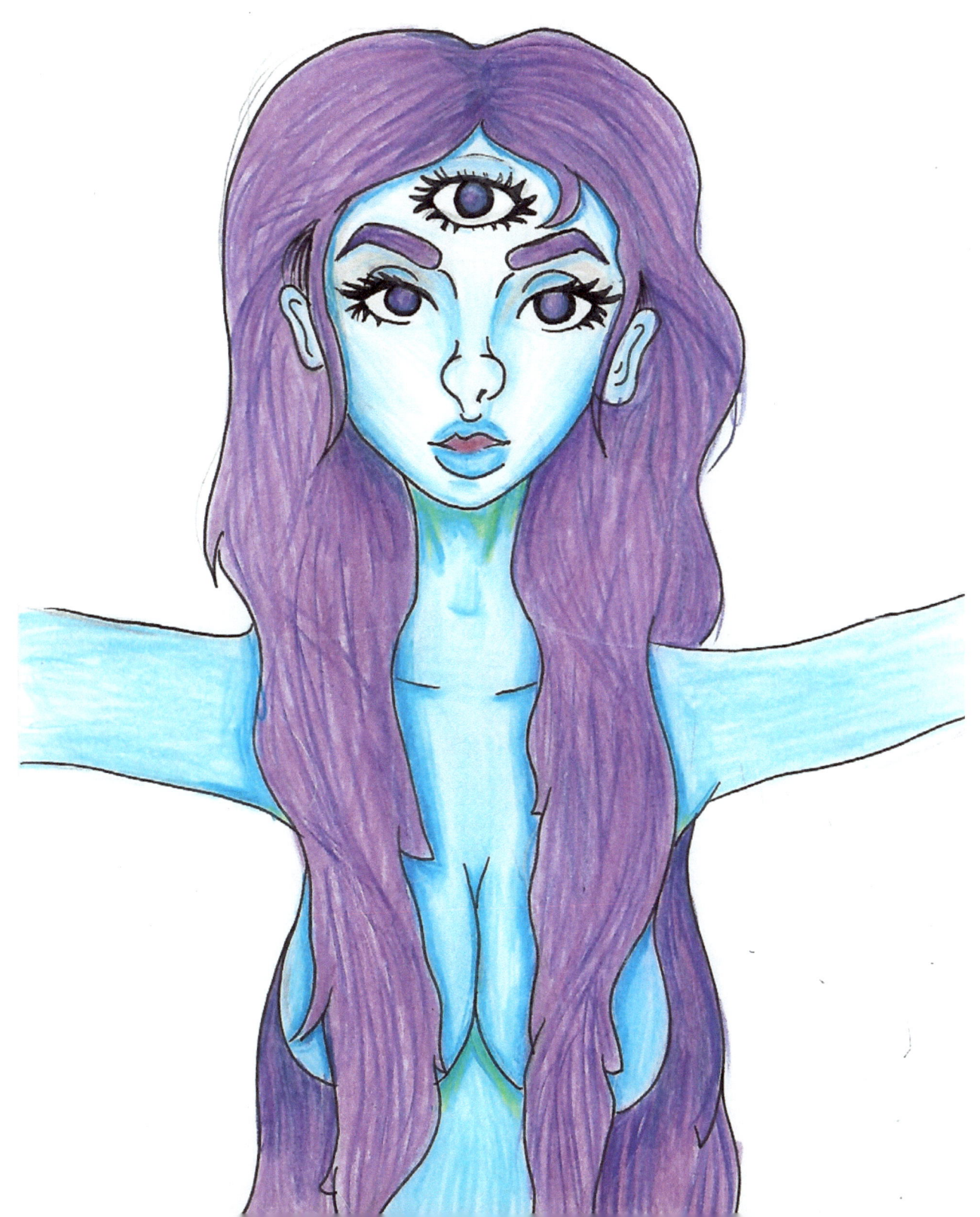

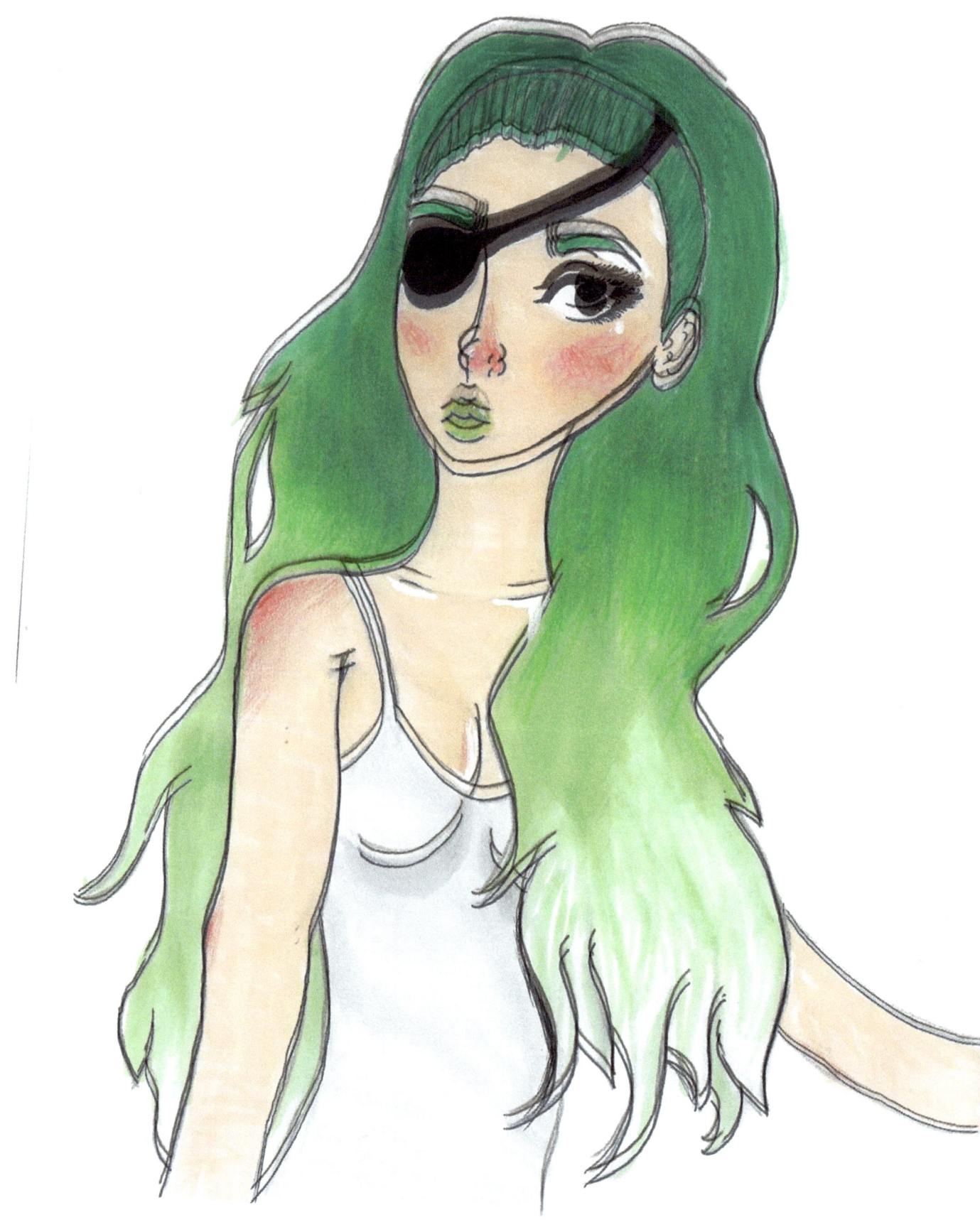

2017

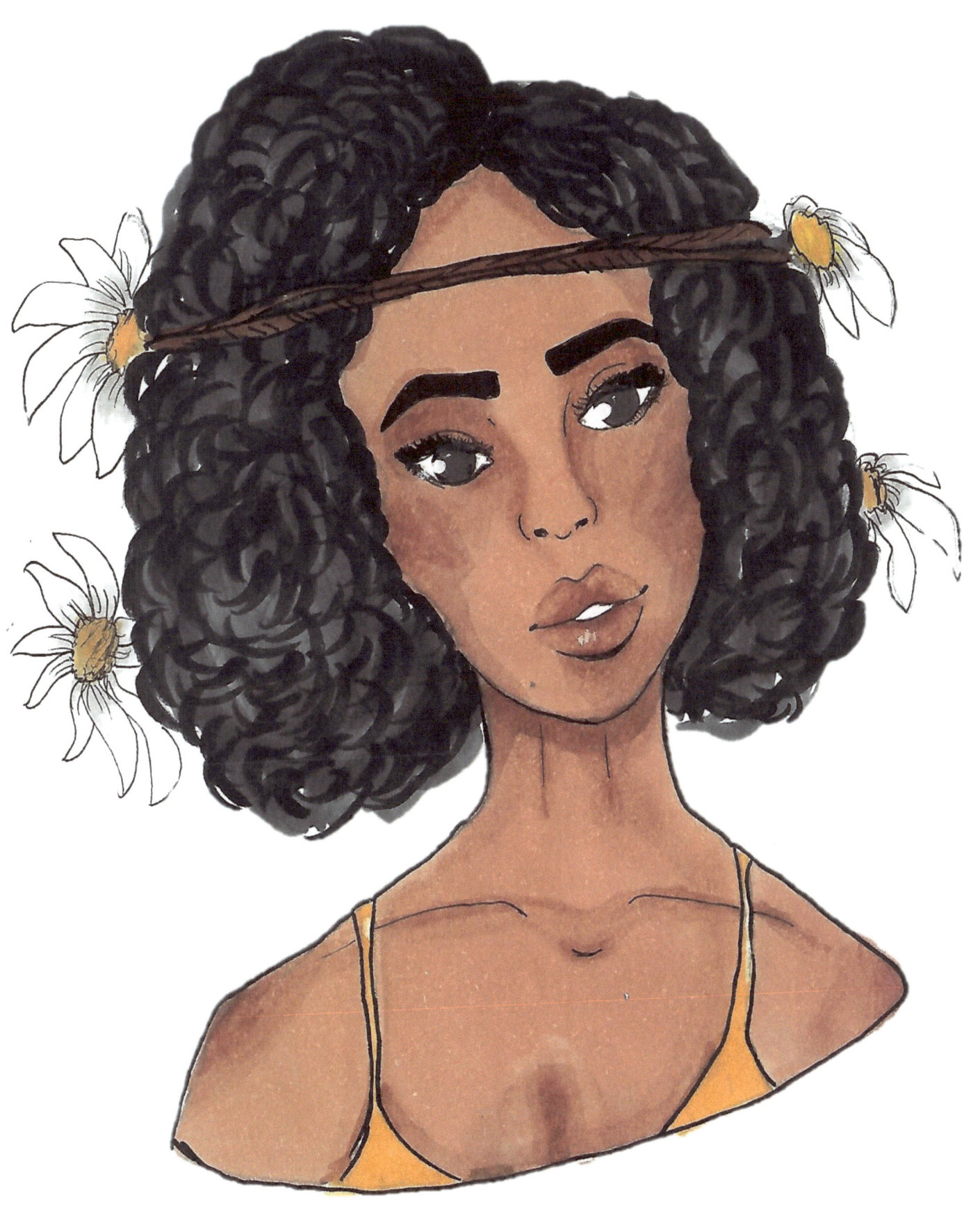

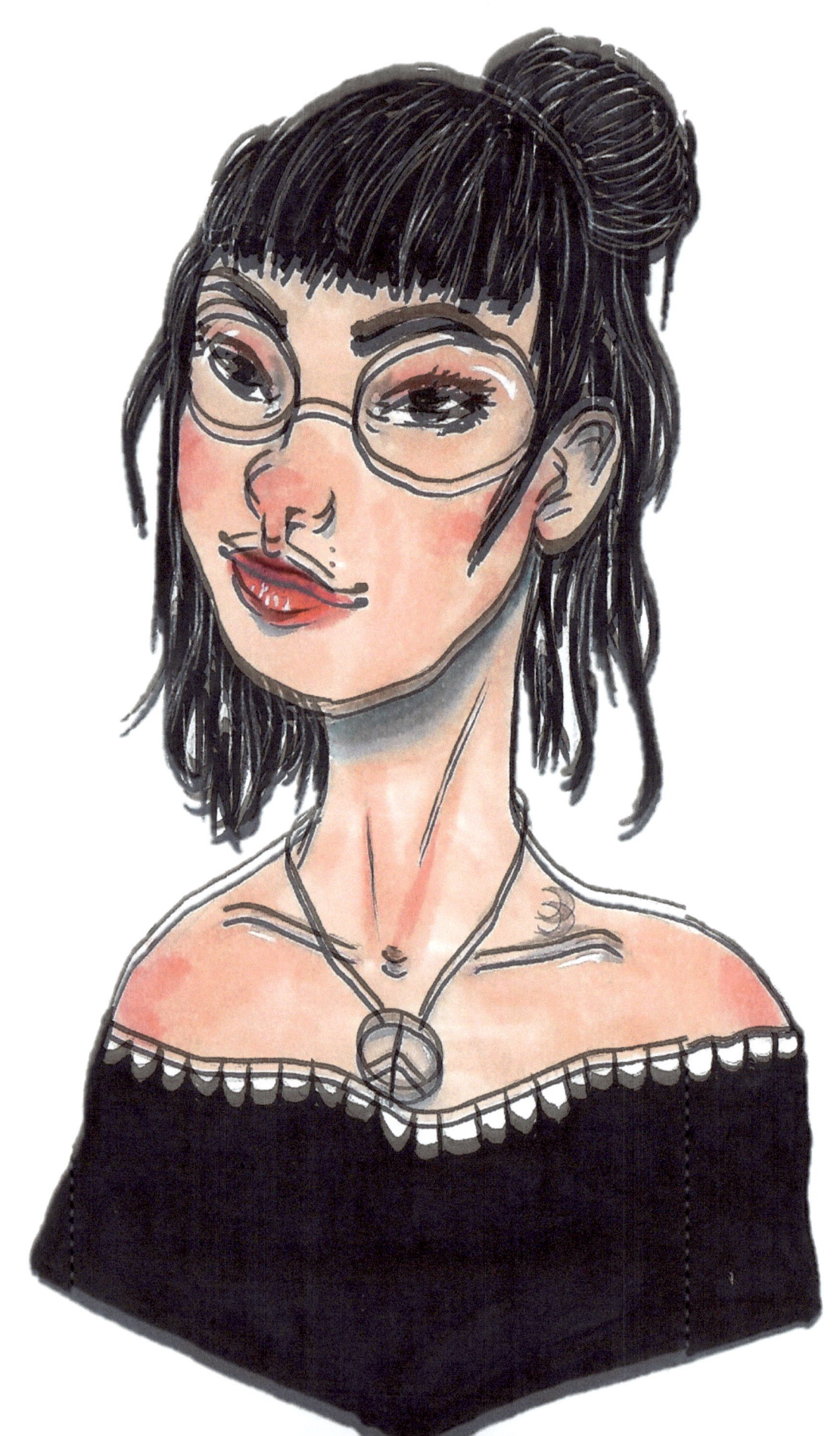

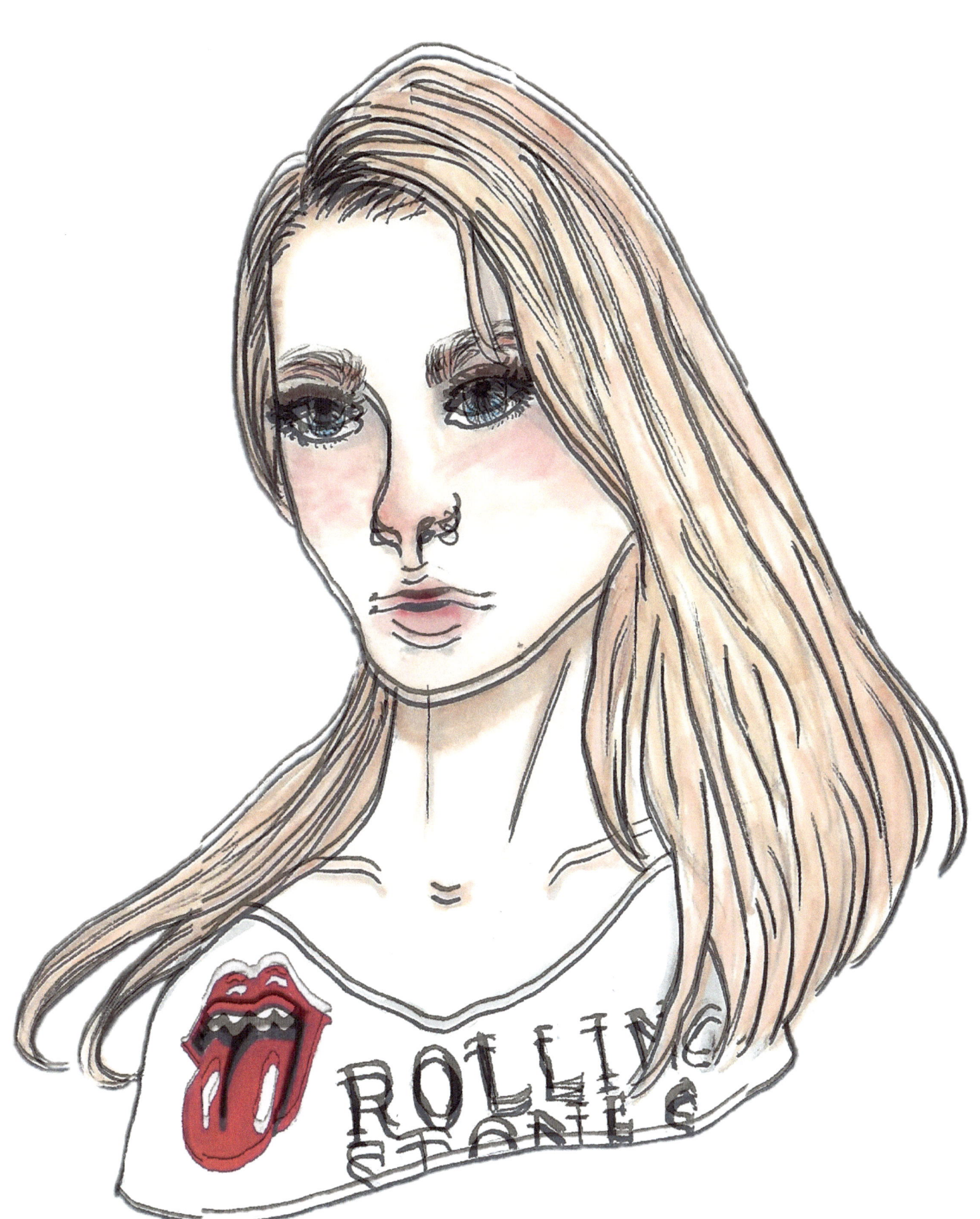

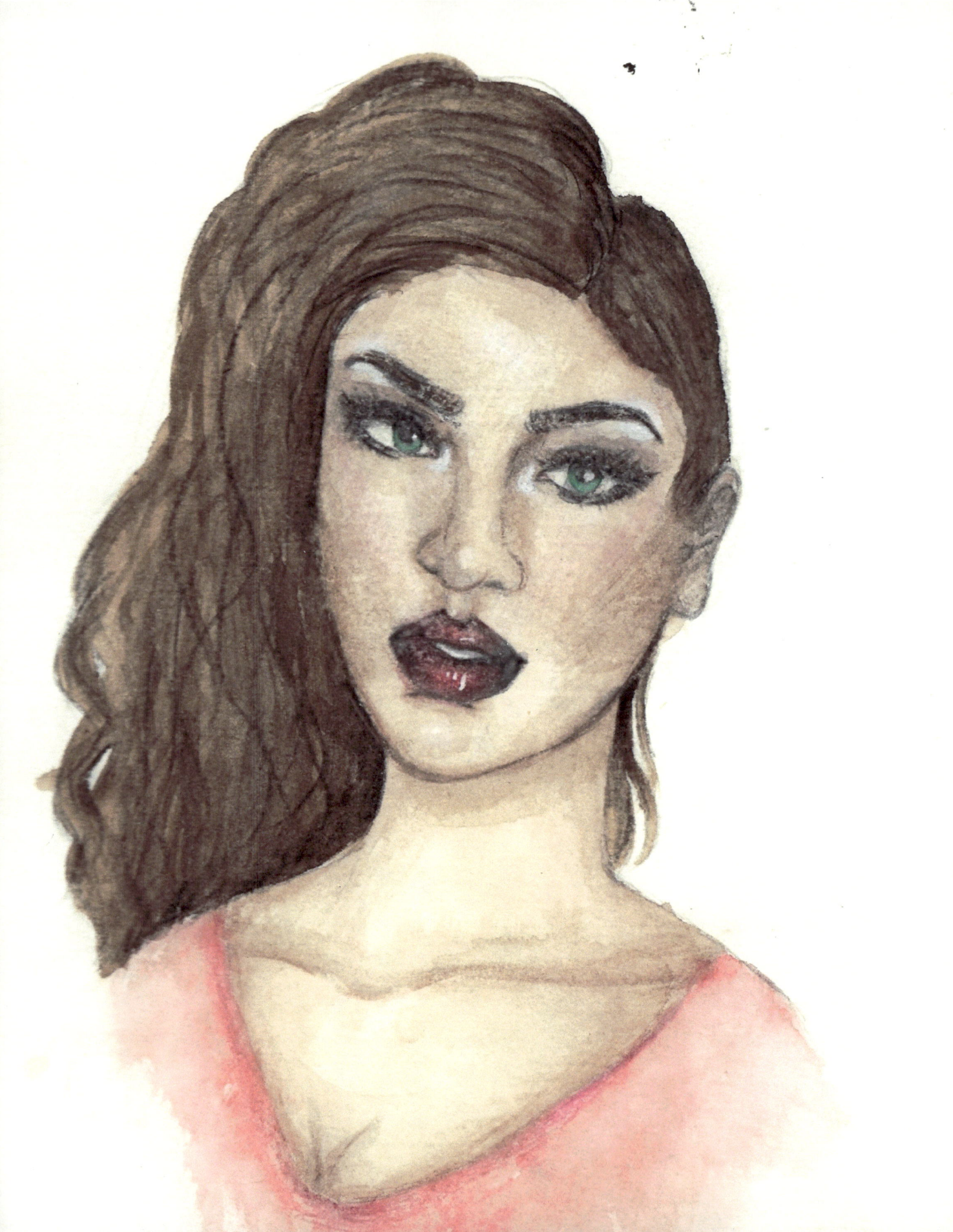

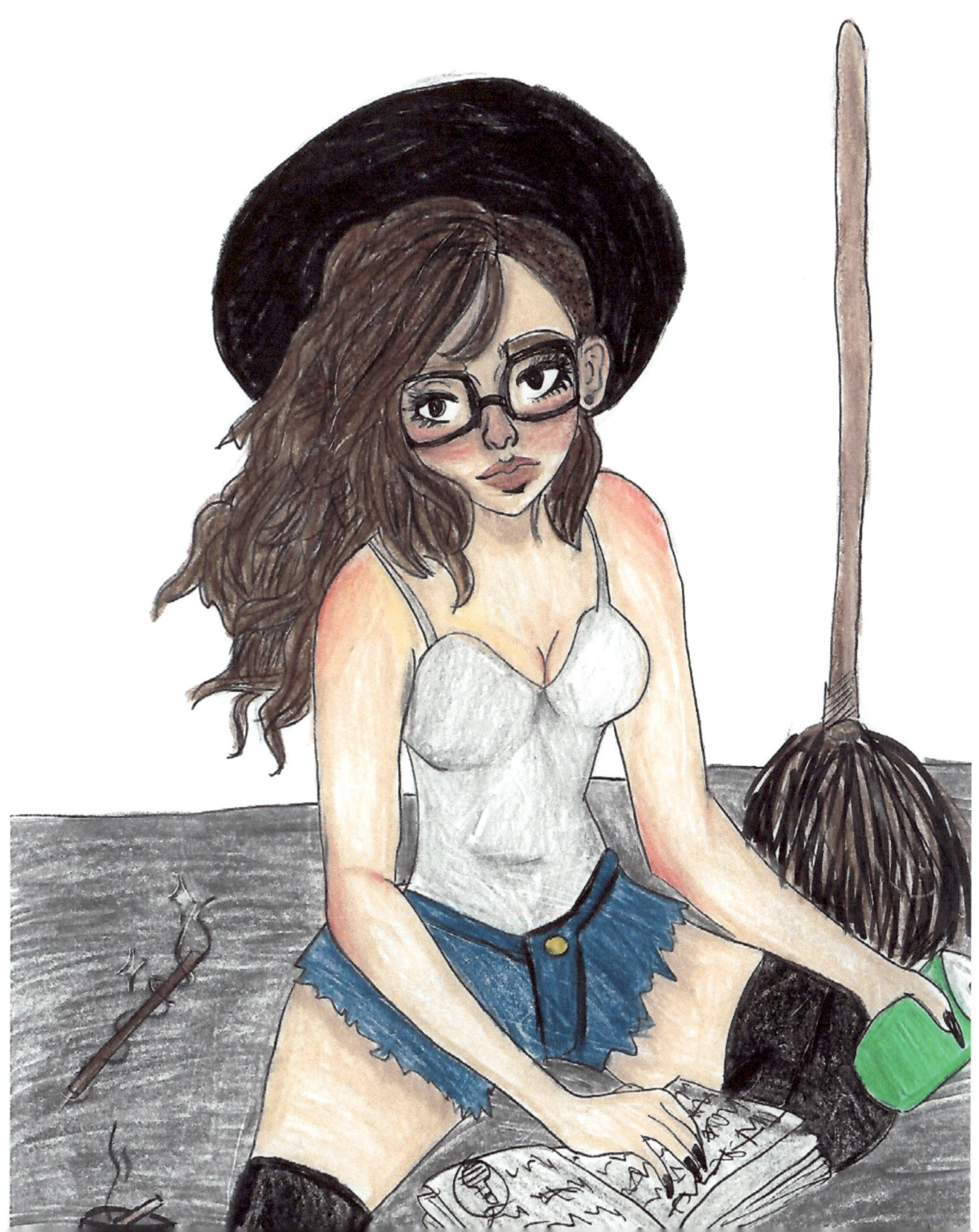

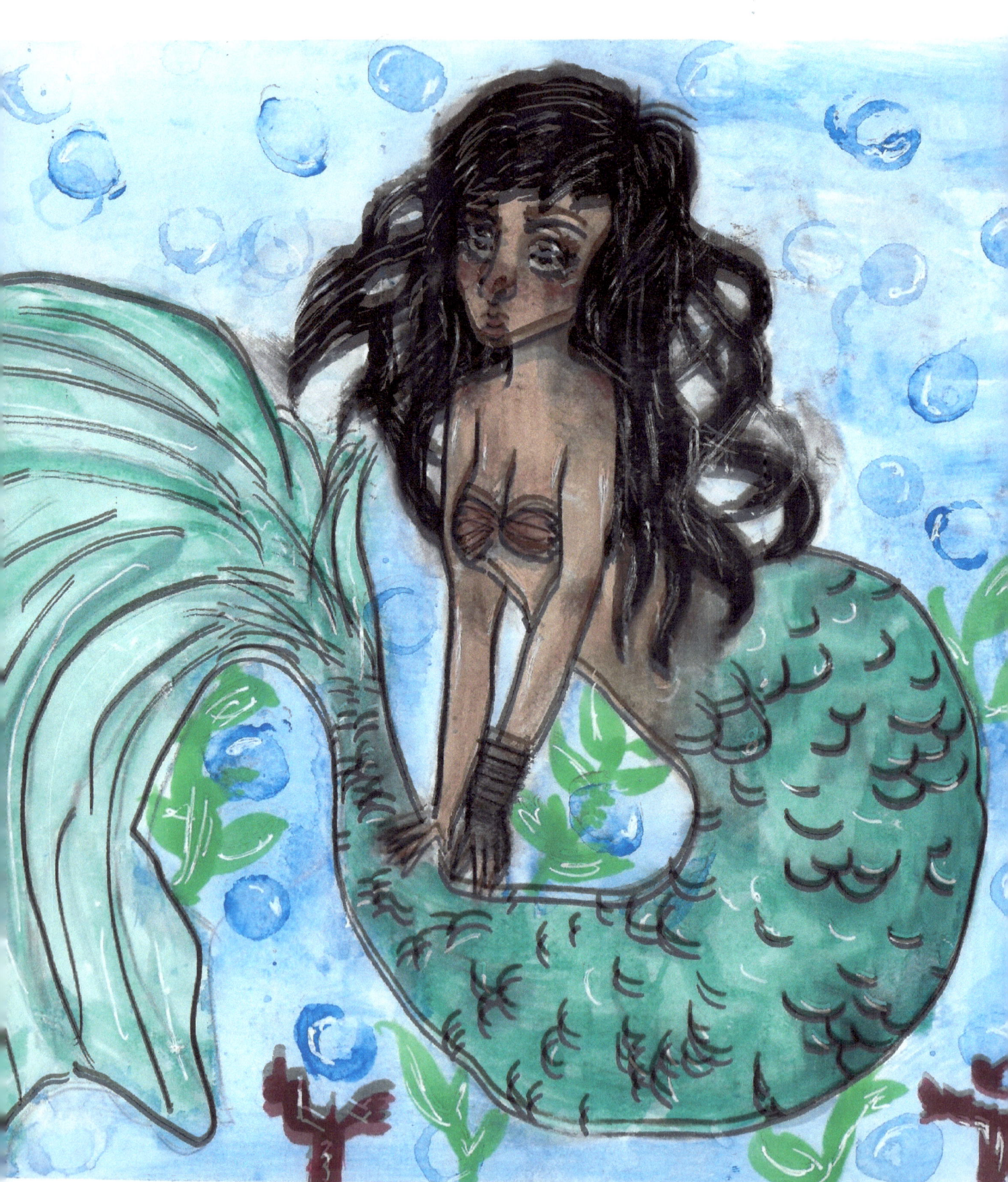

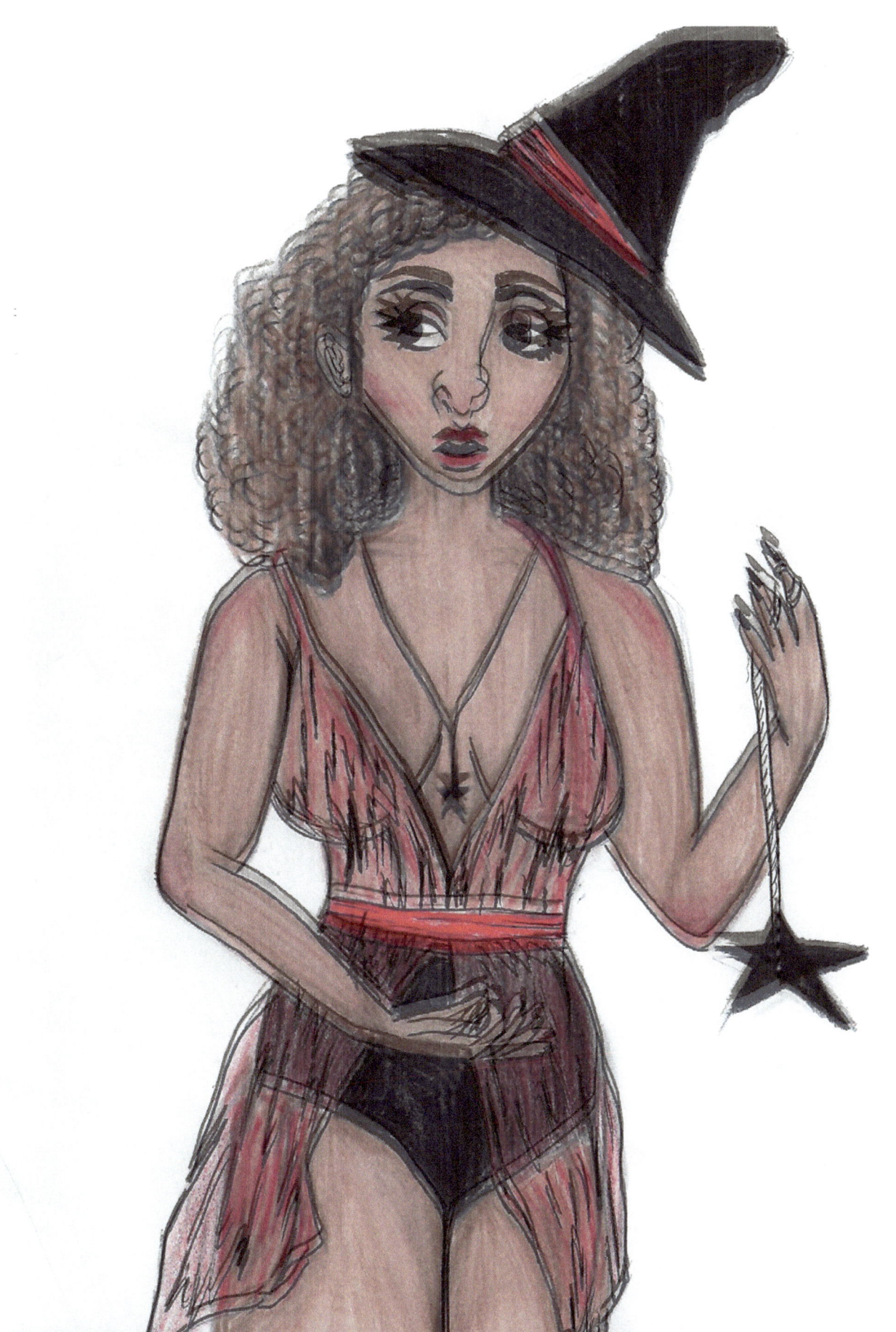

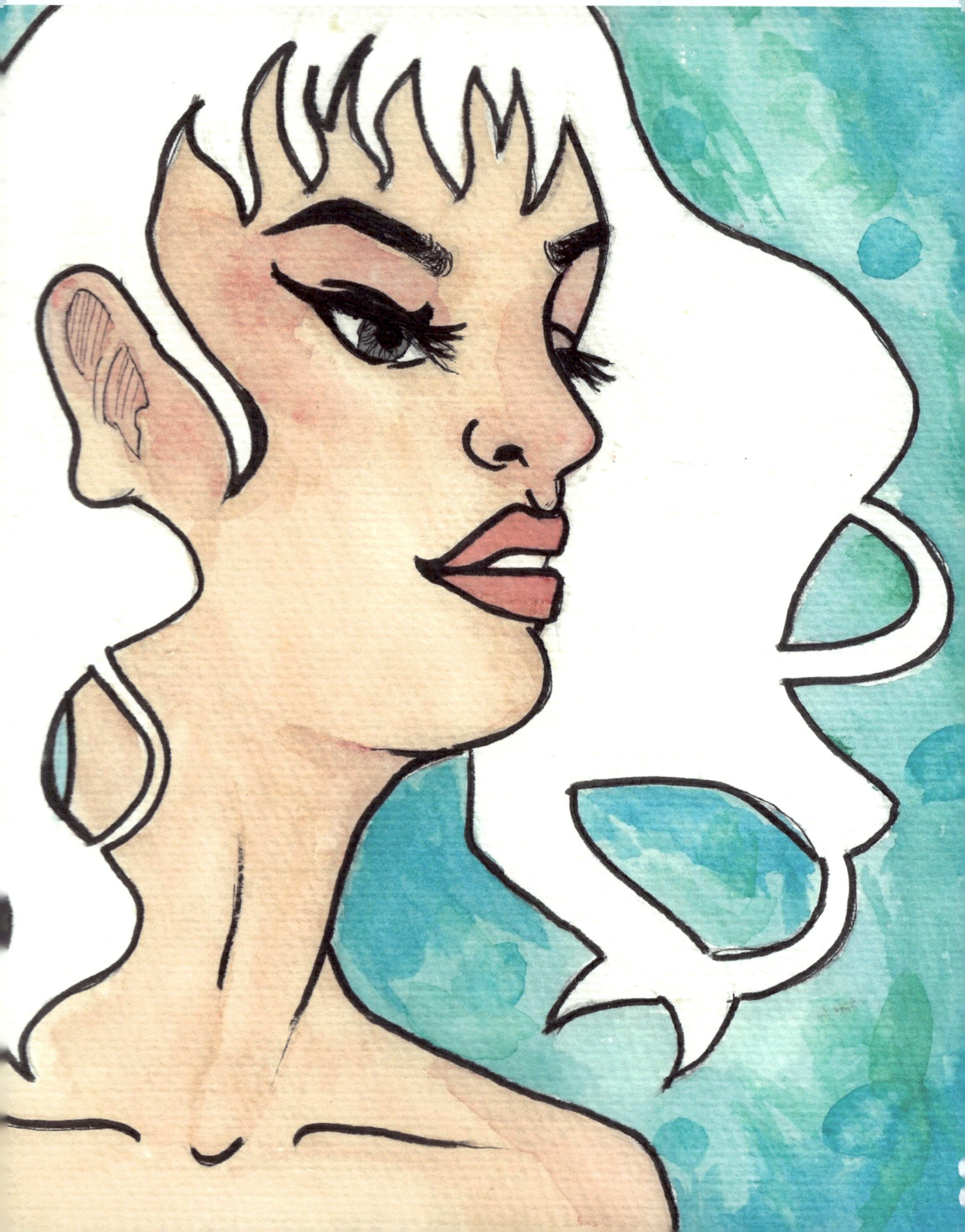

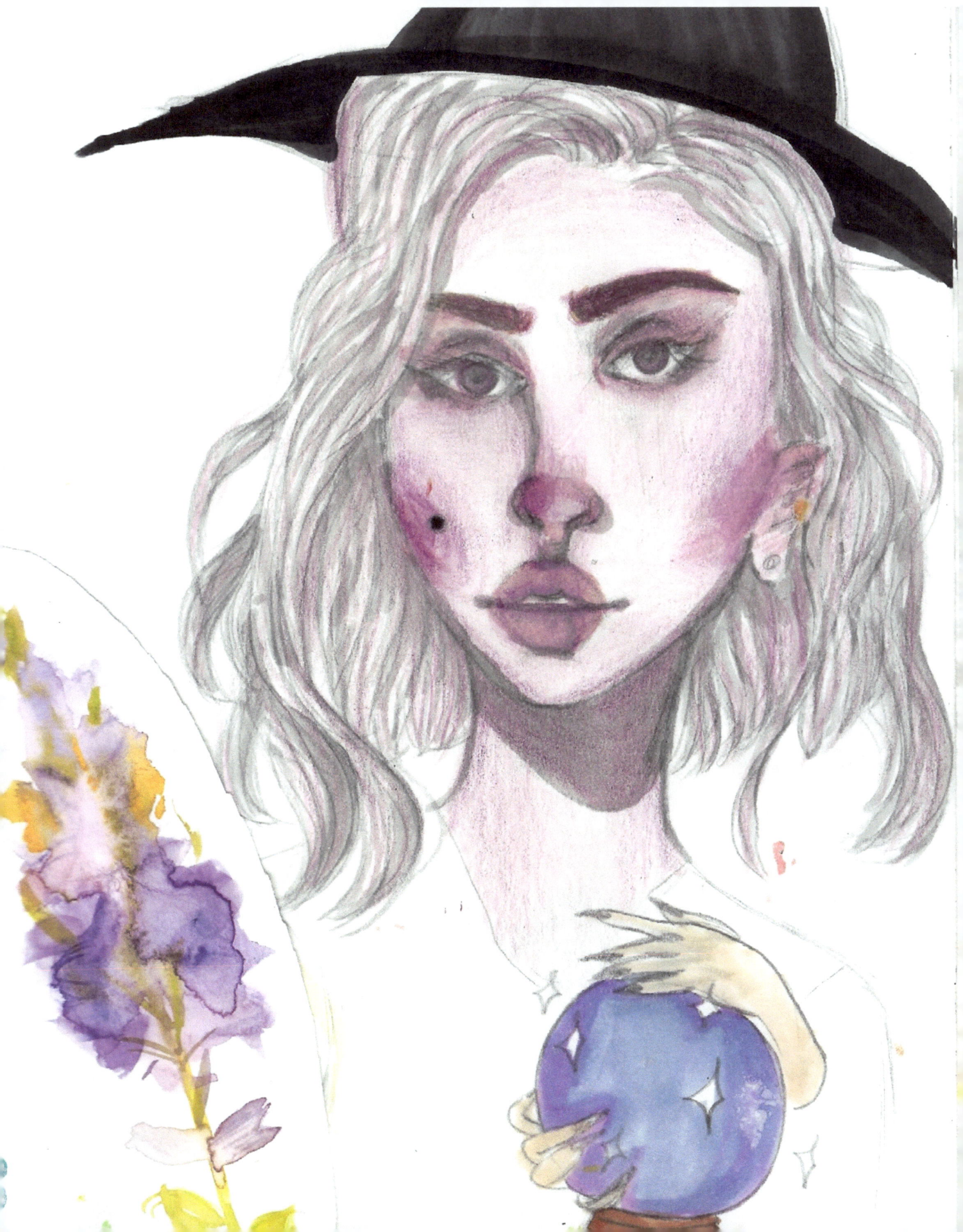

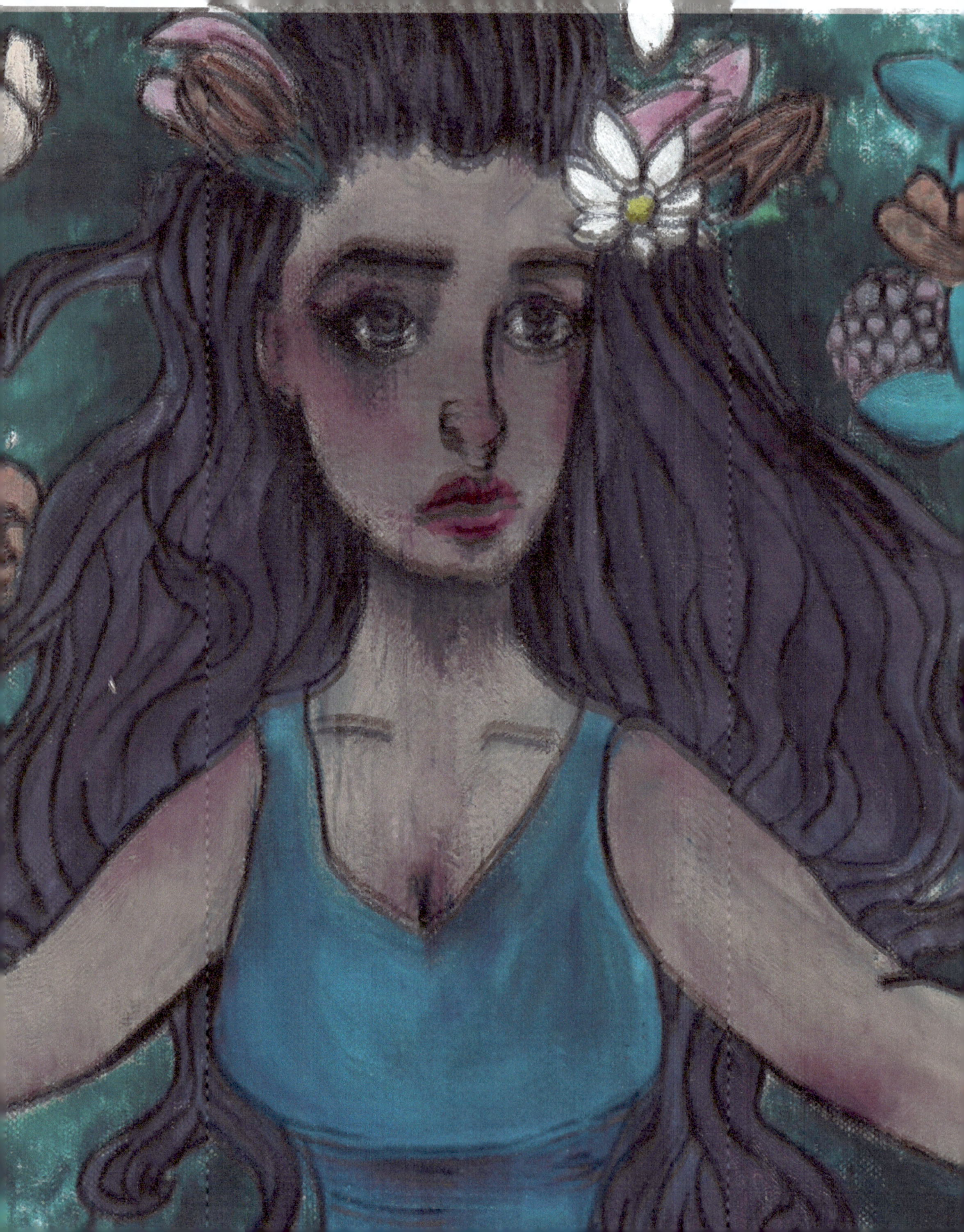

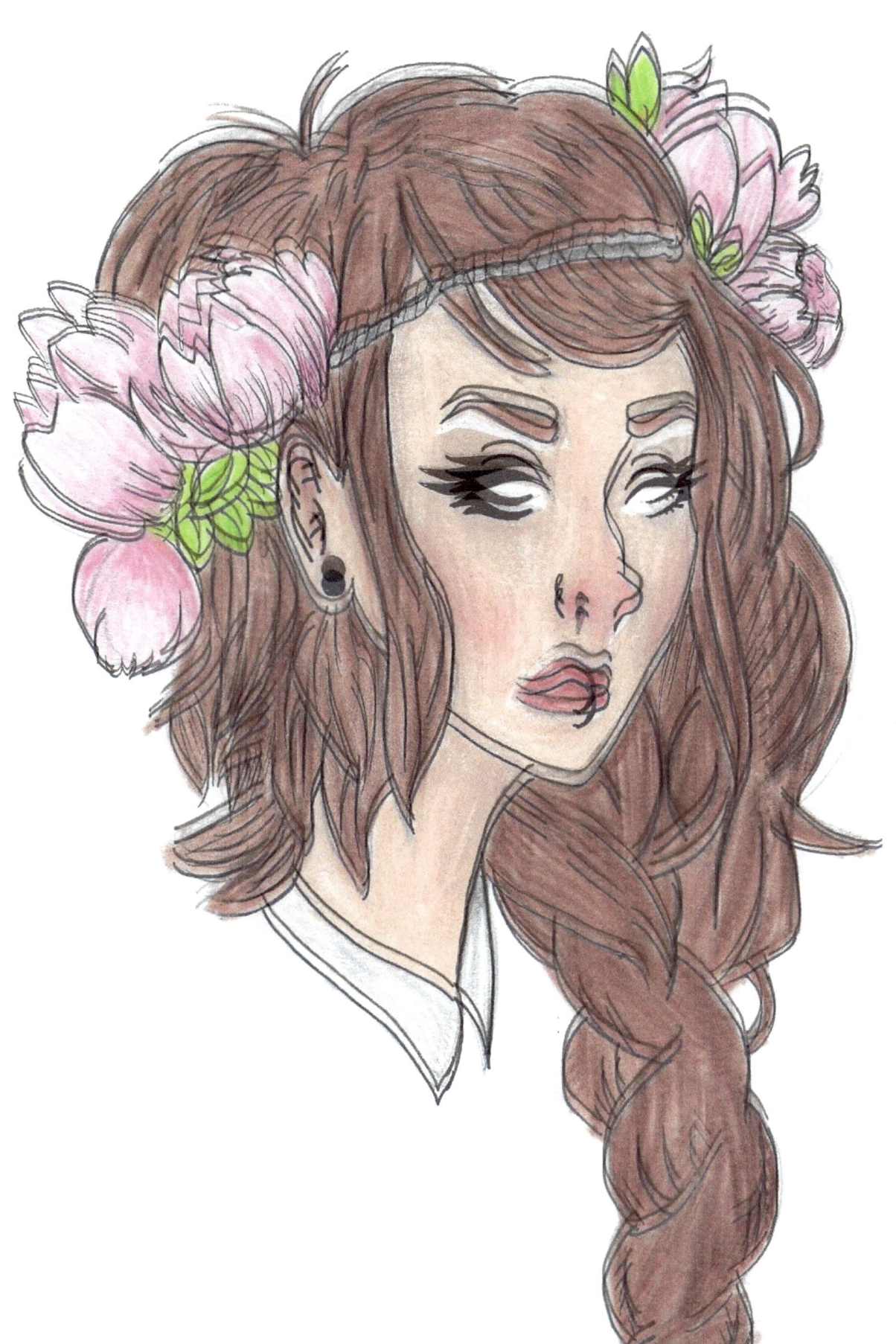

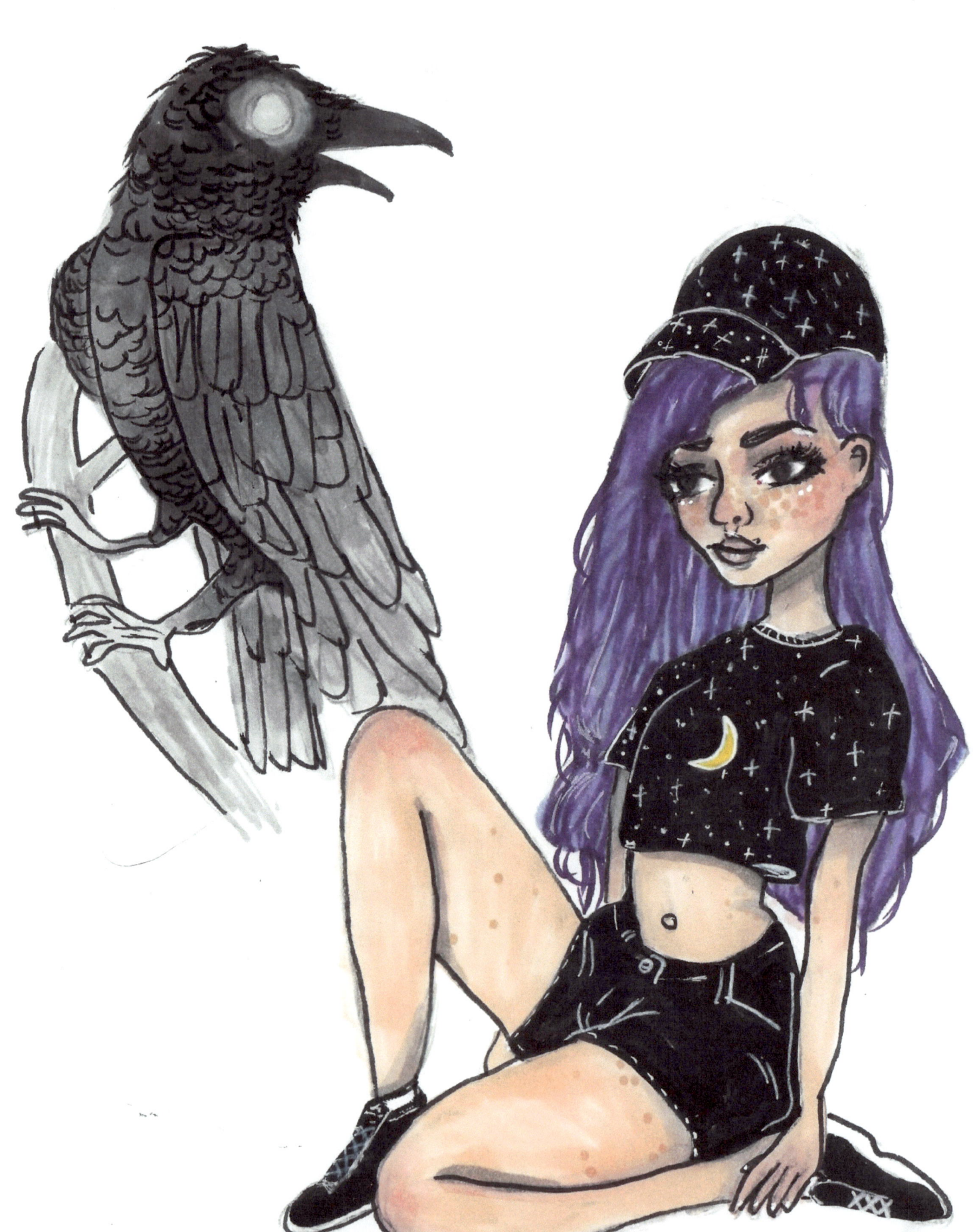

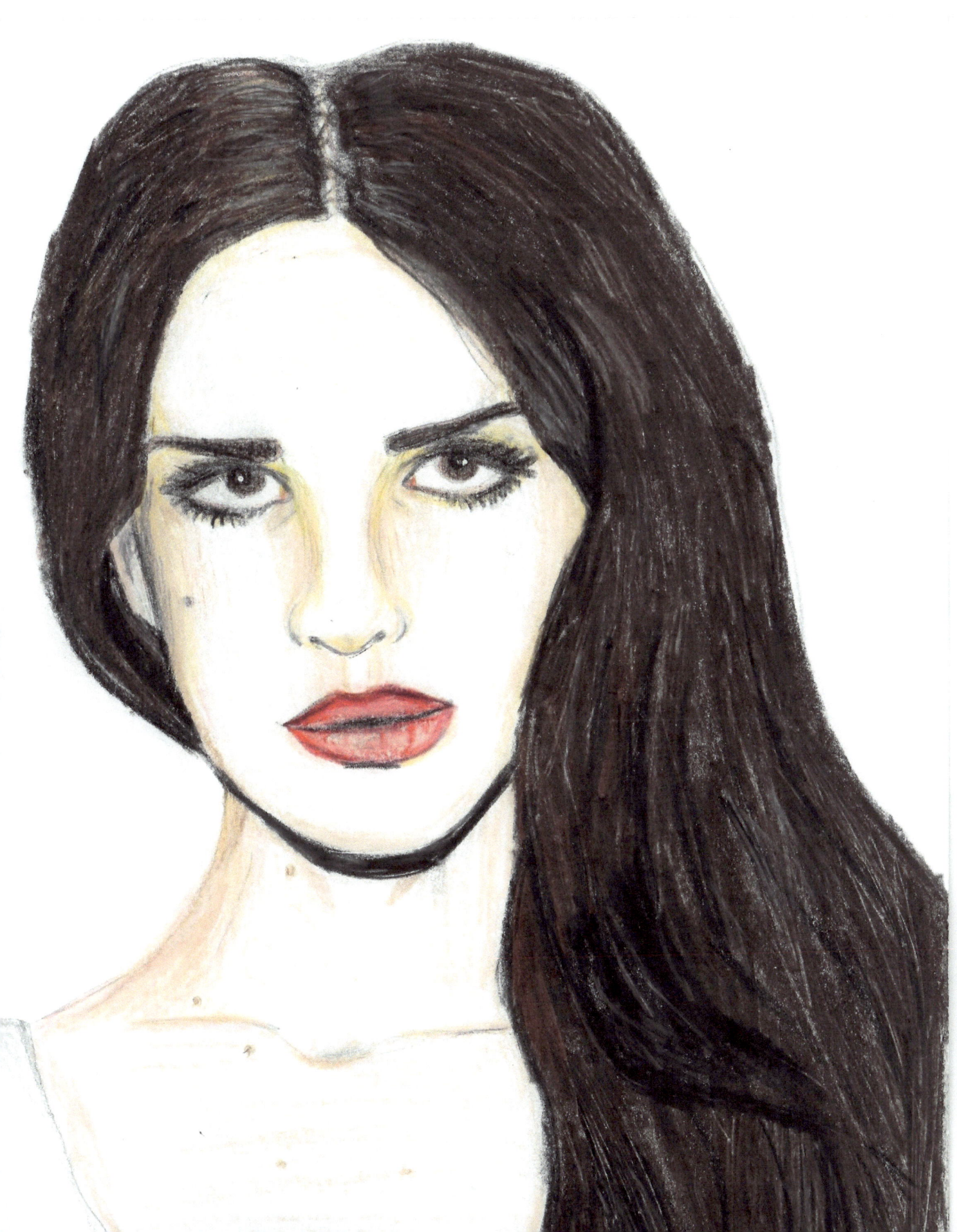

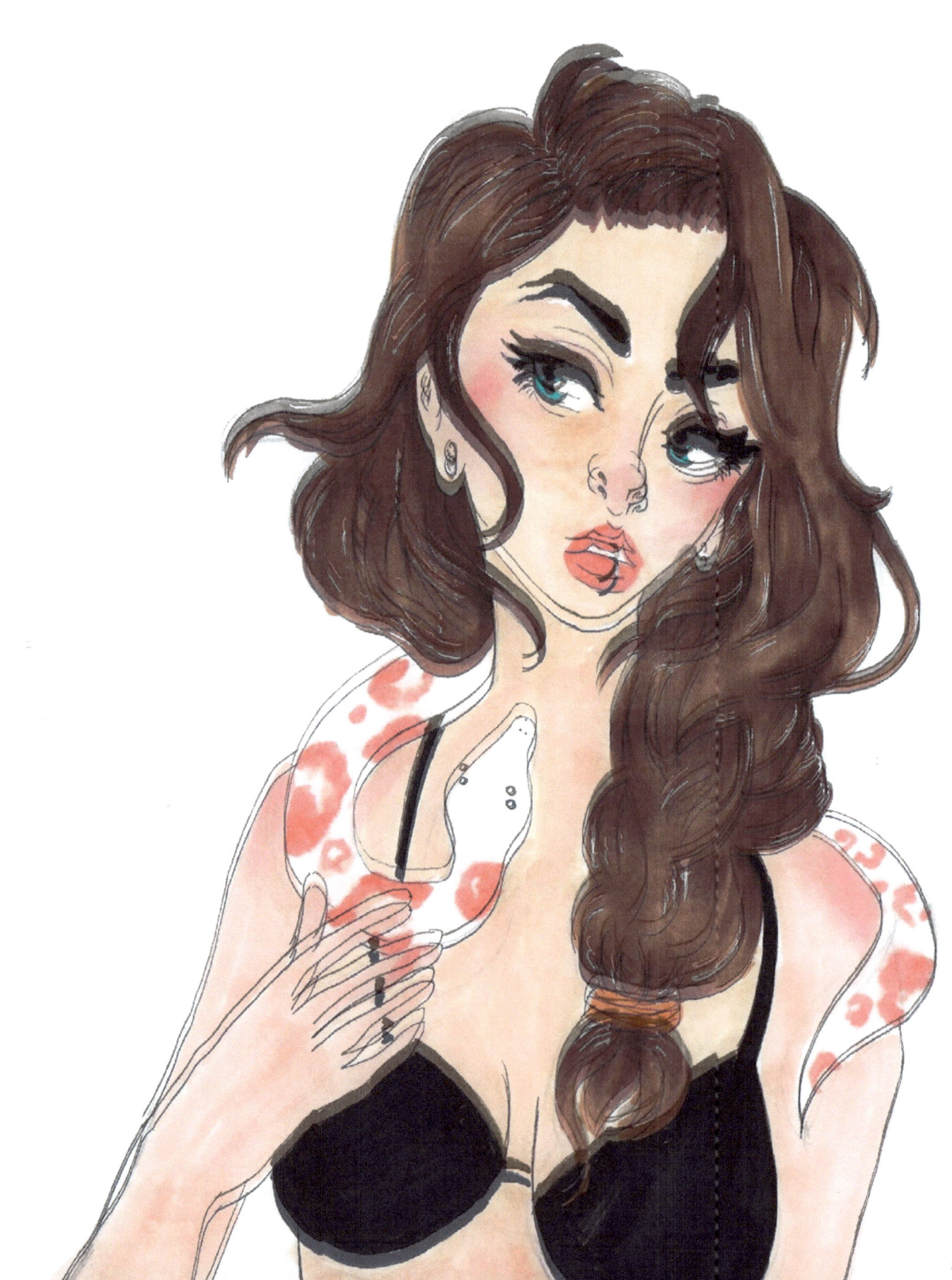

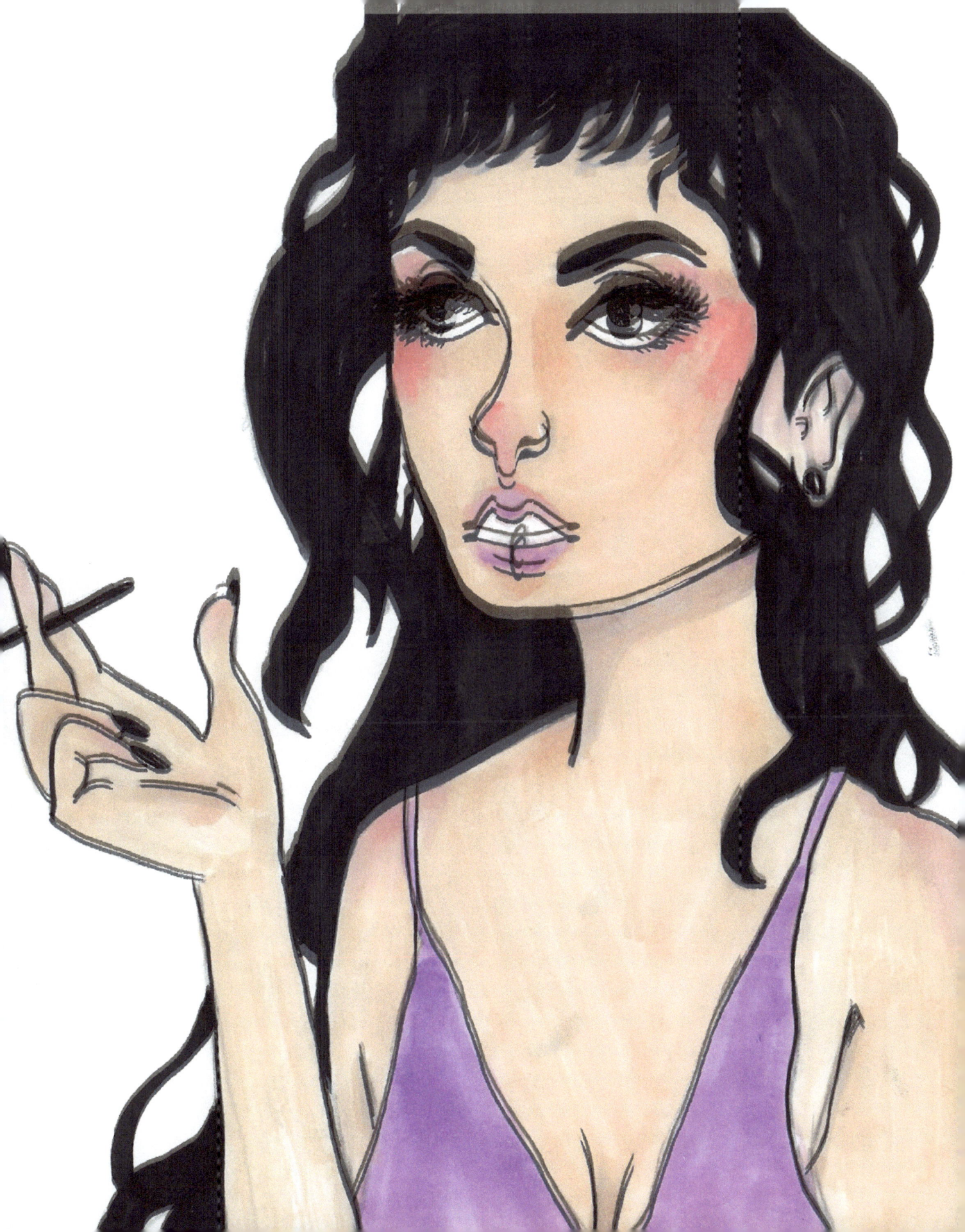

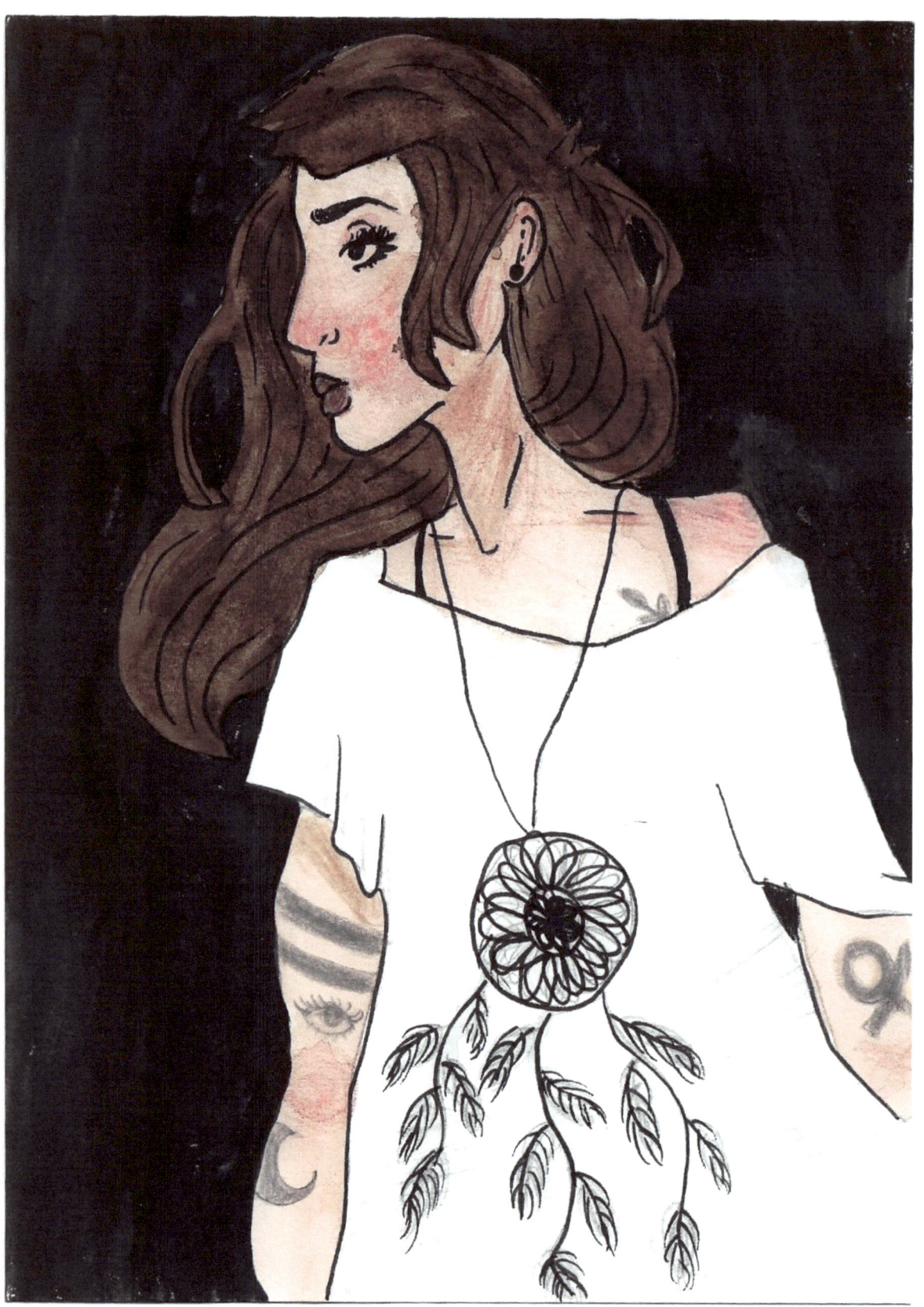

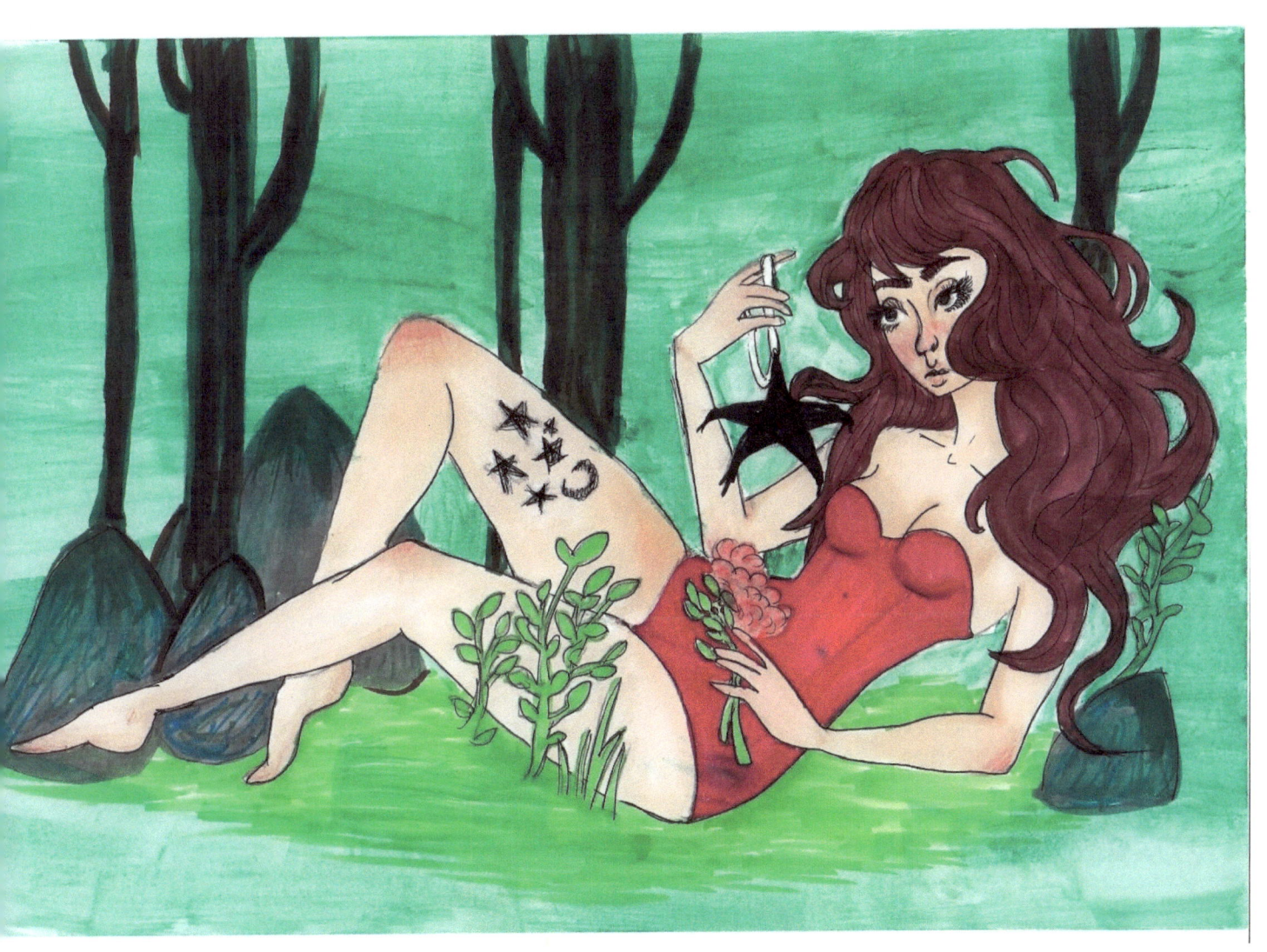

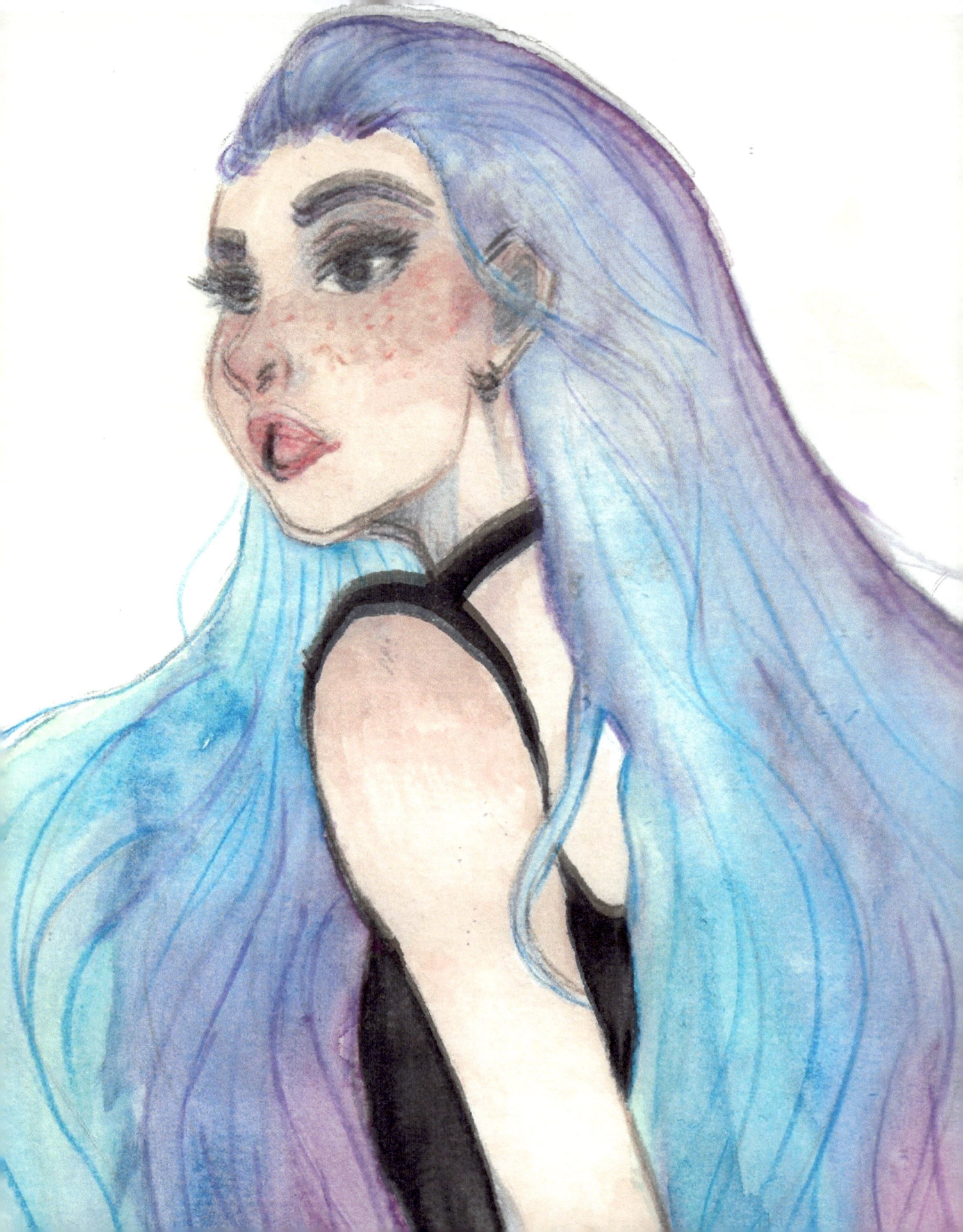

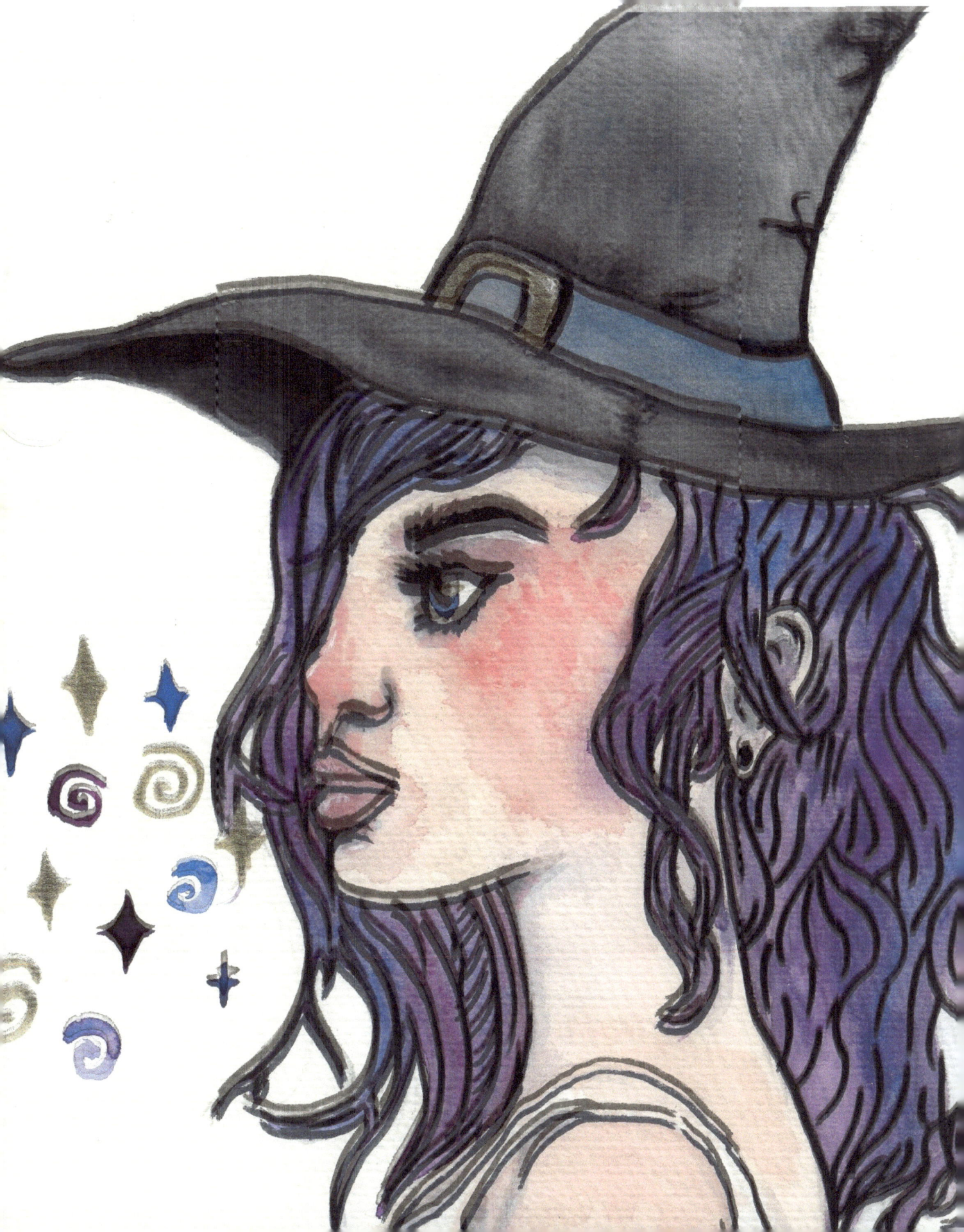

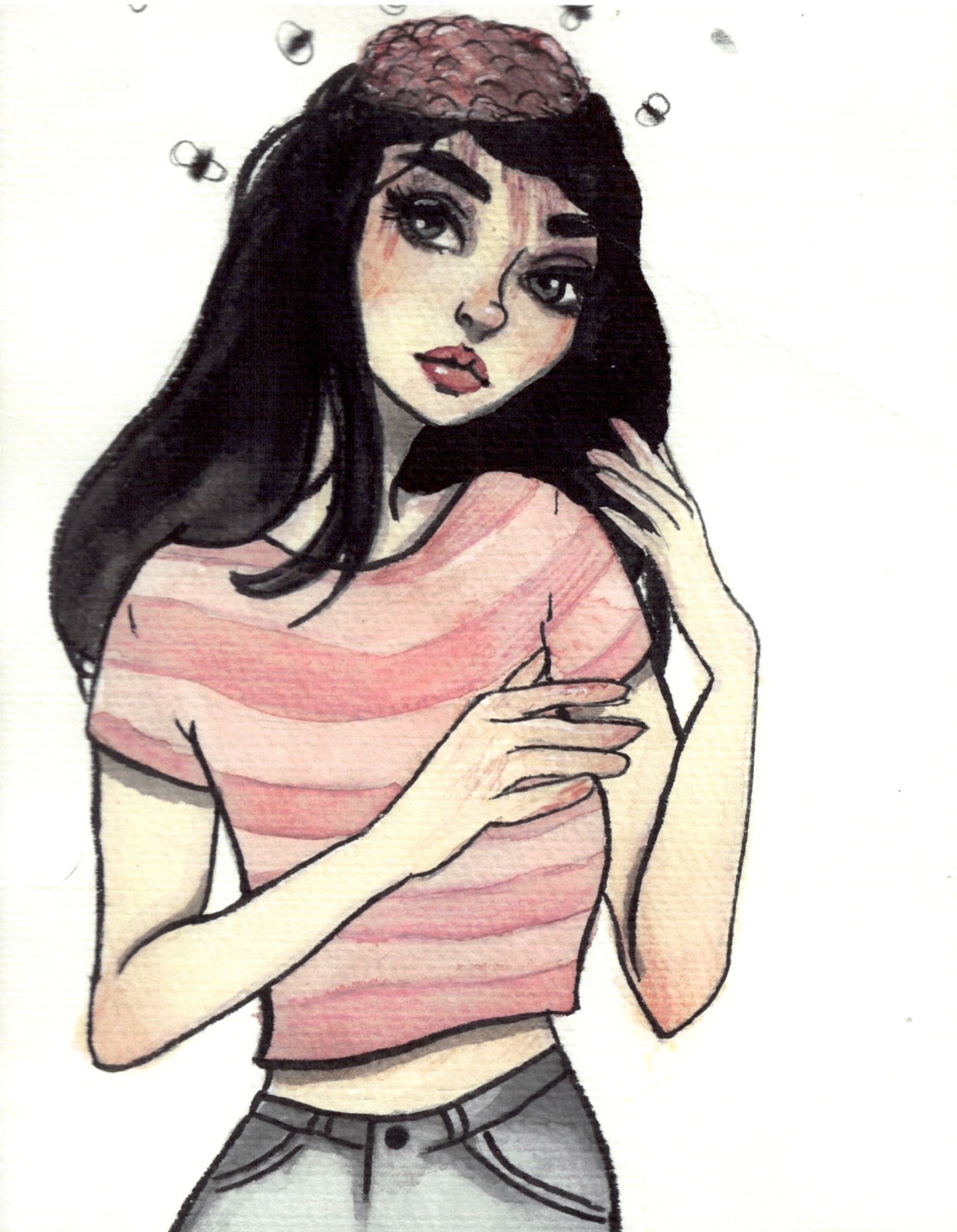

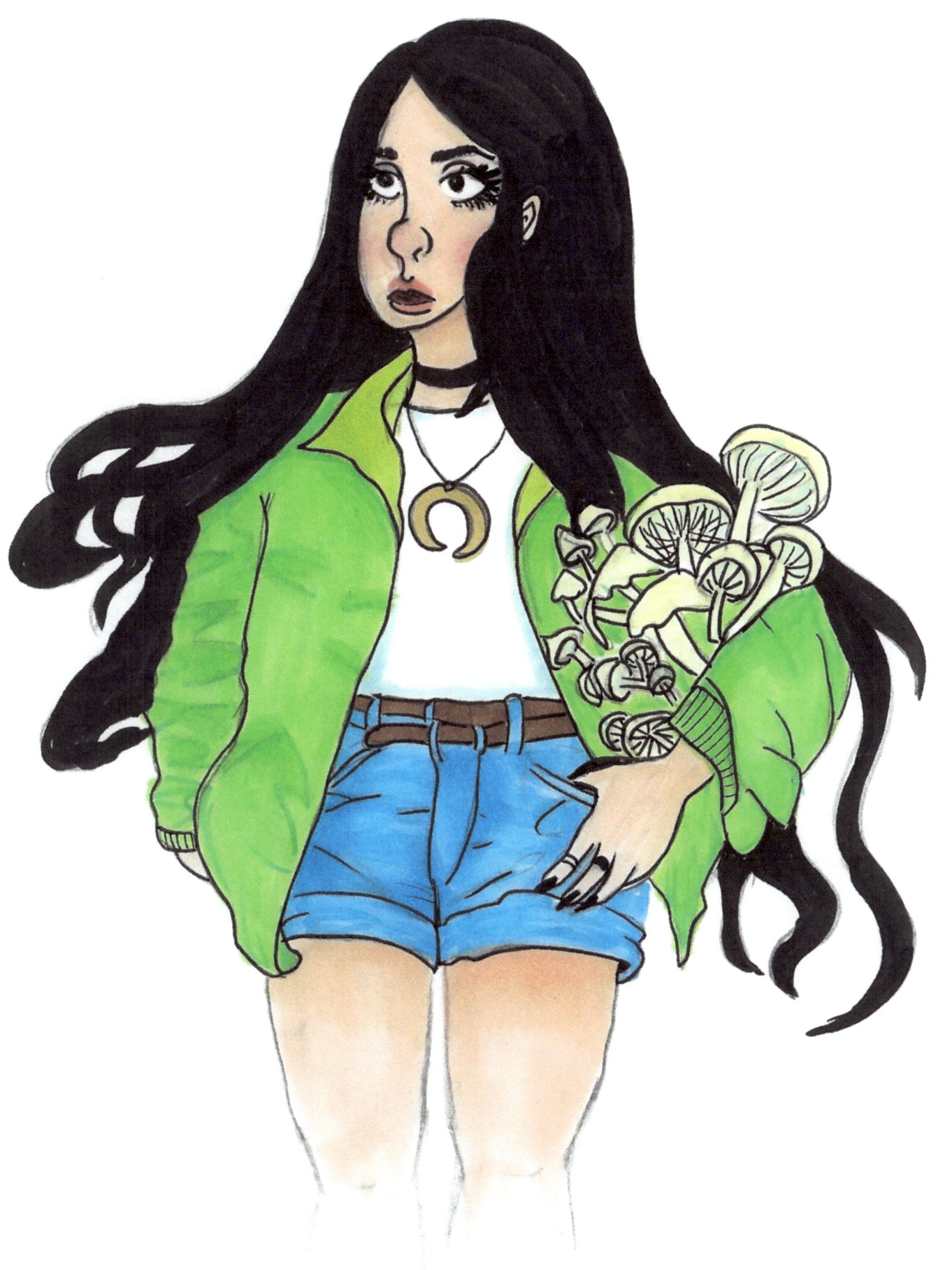

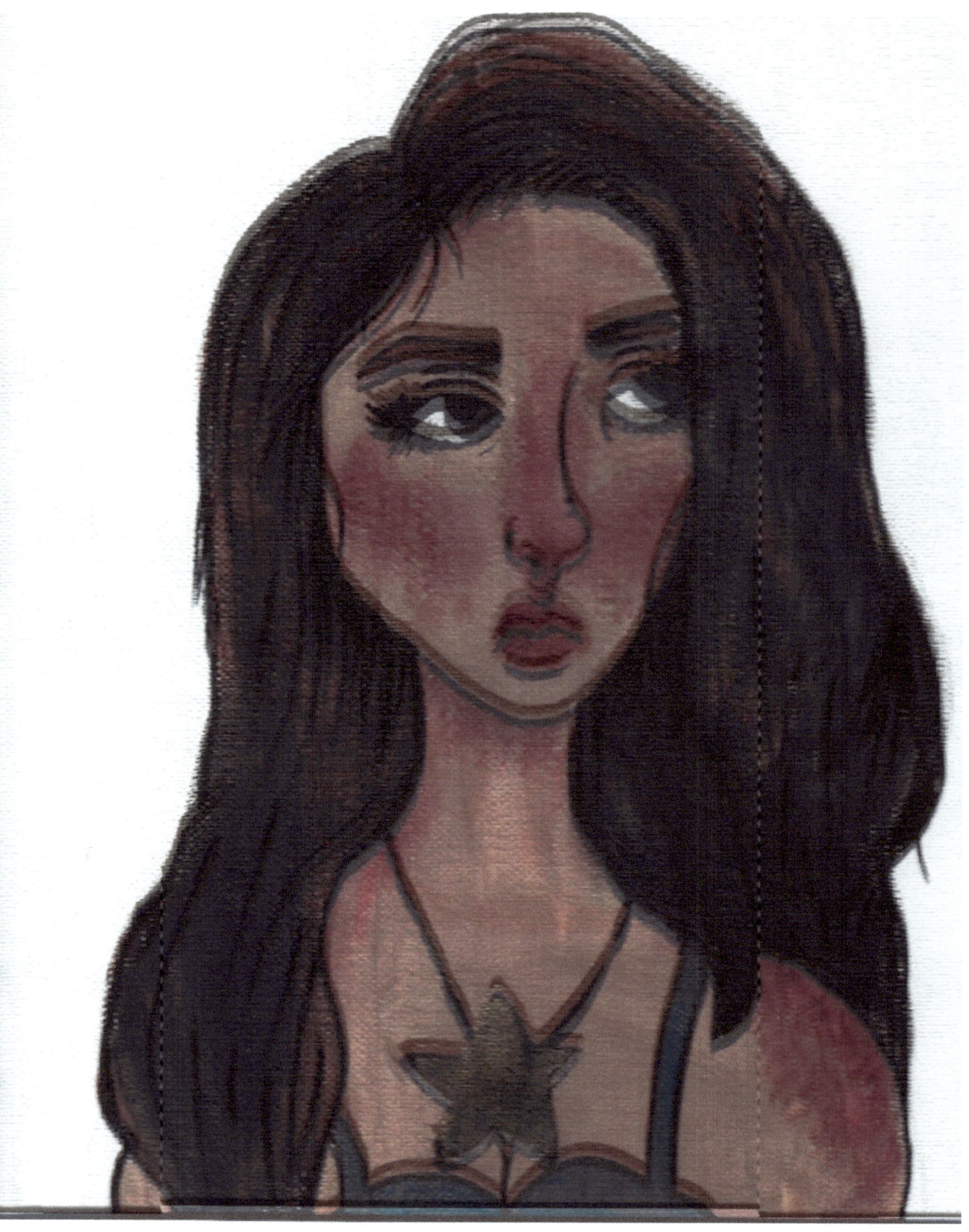

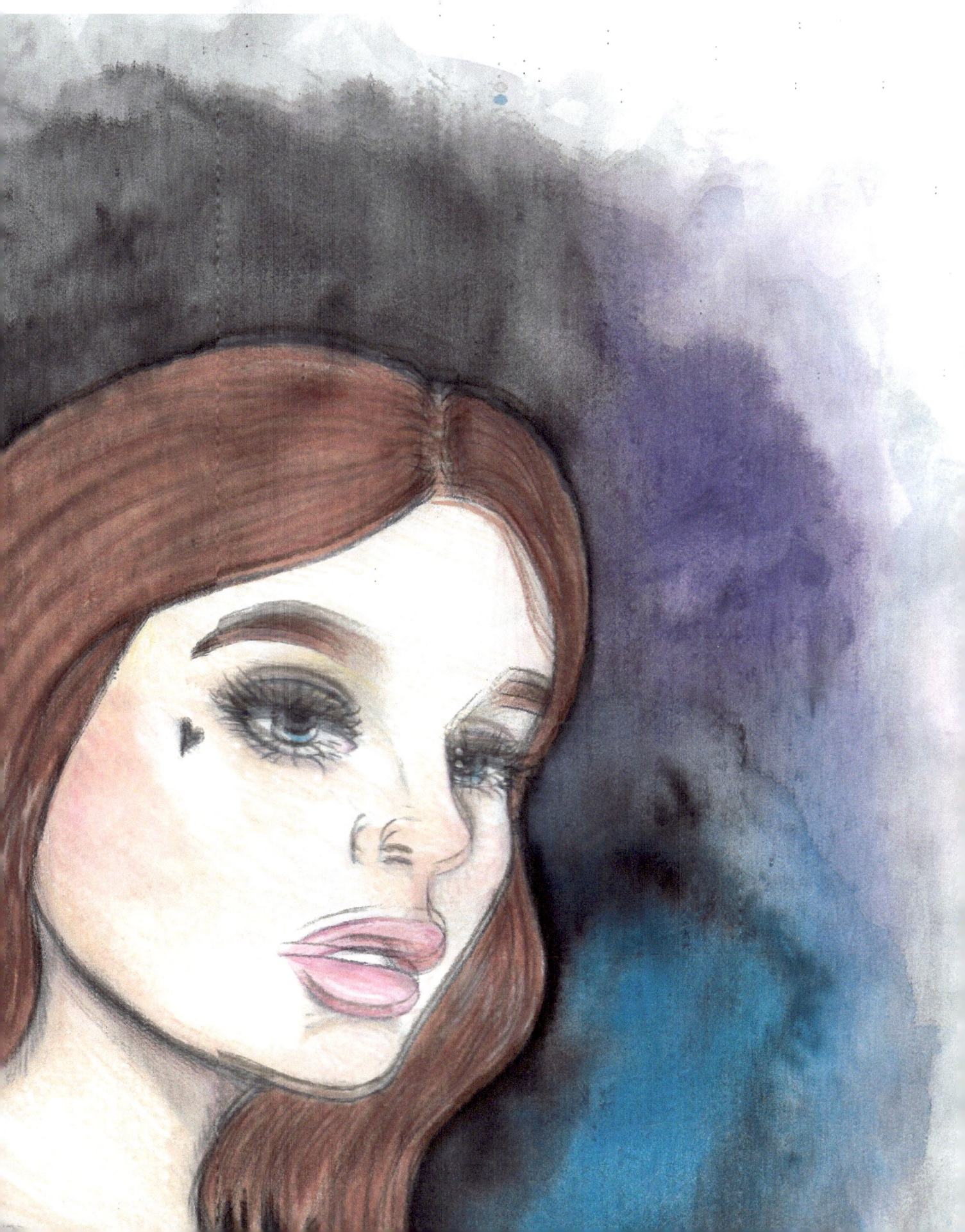

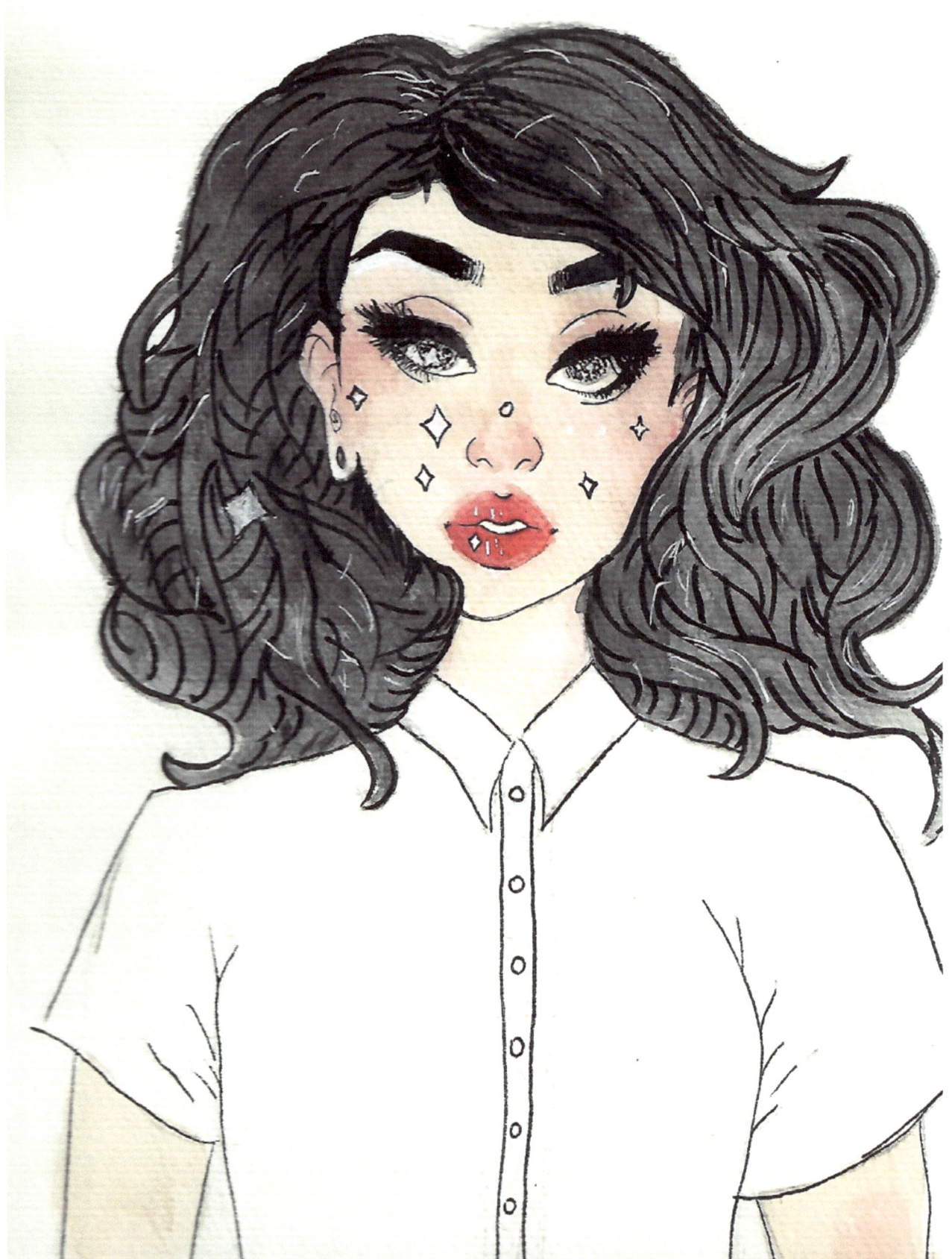

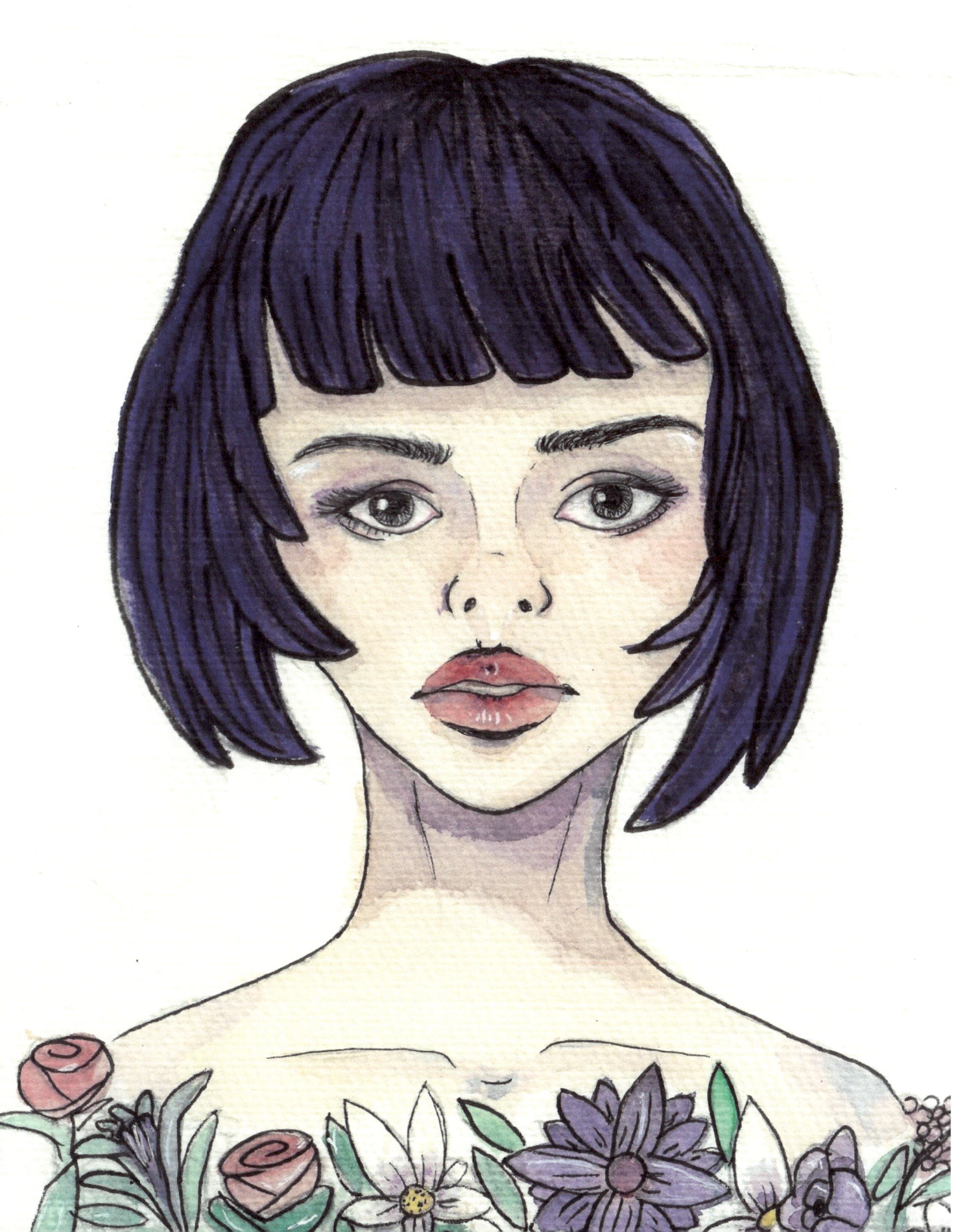

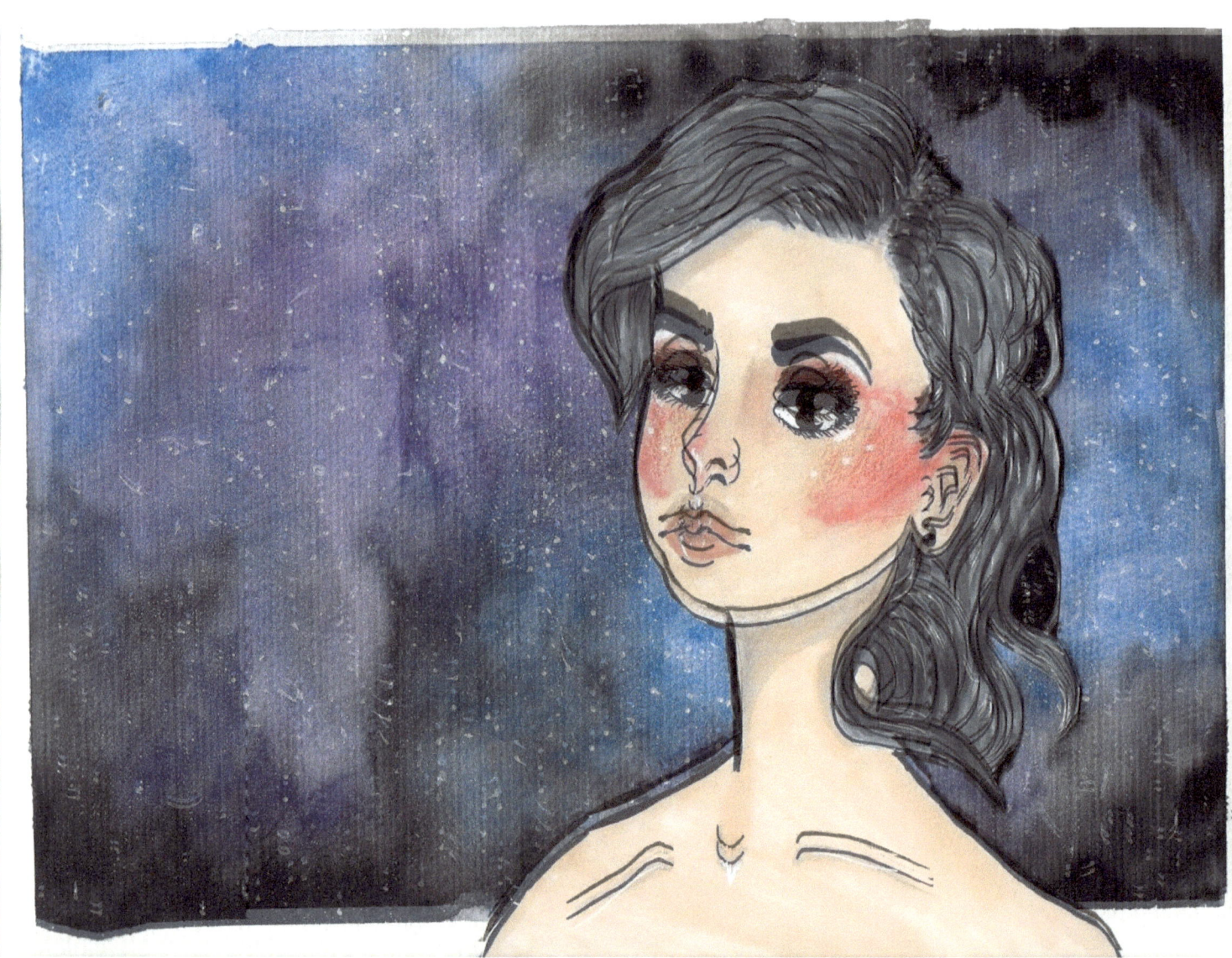

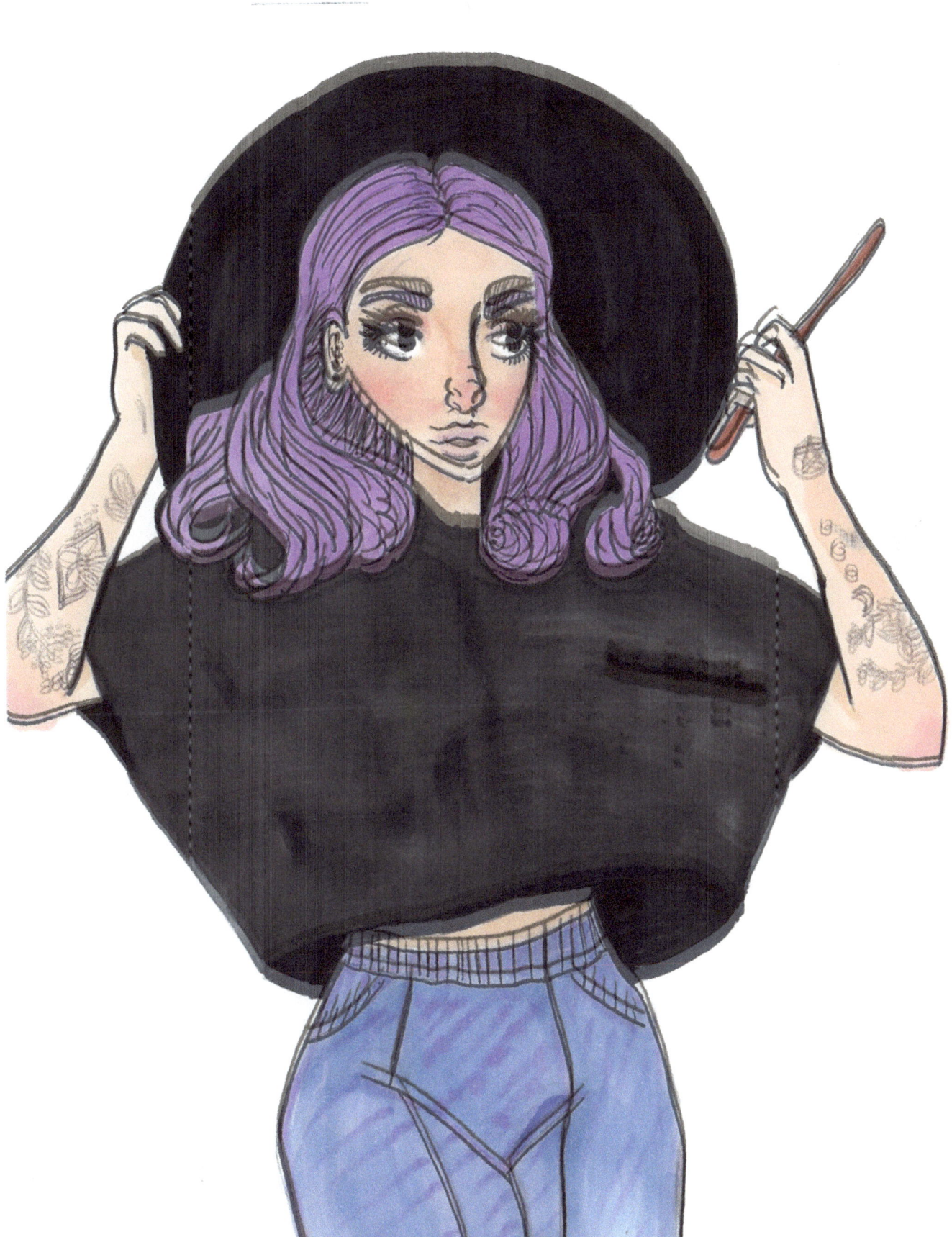

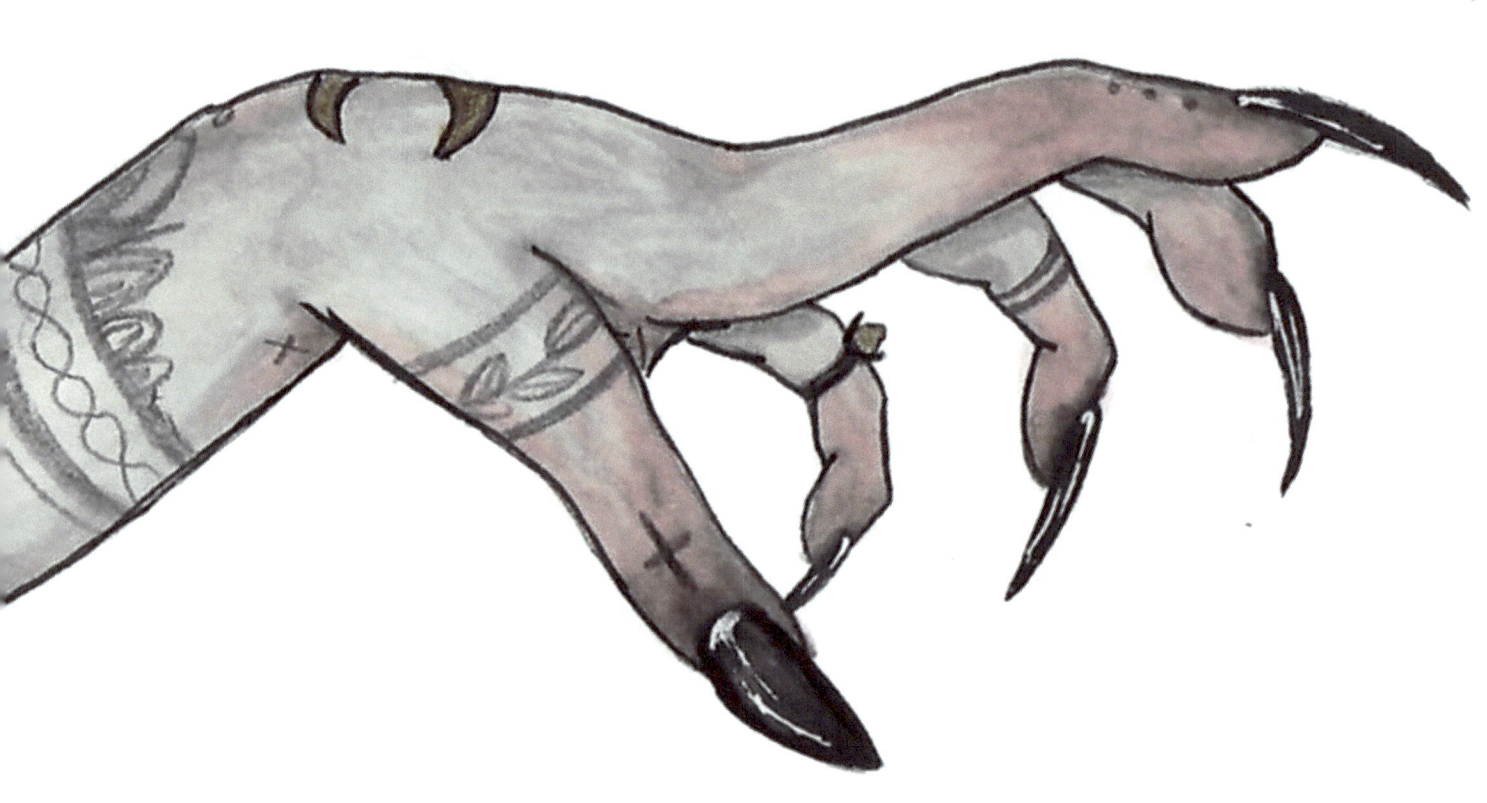

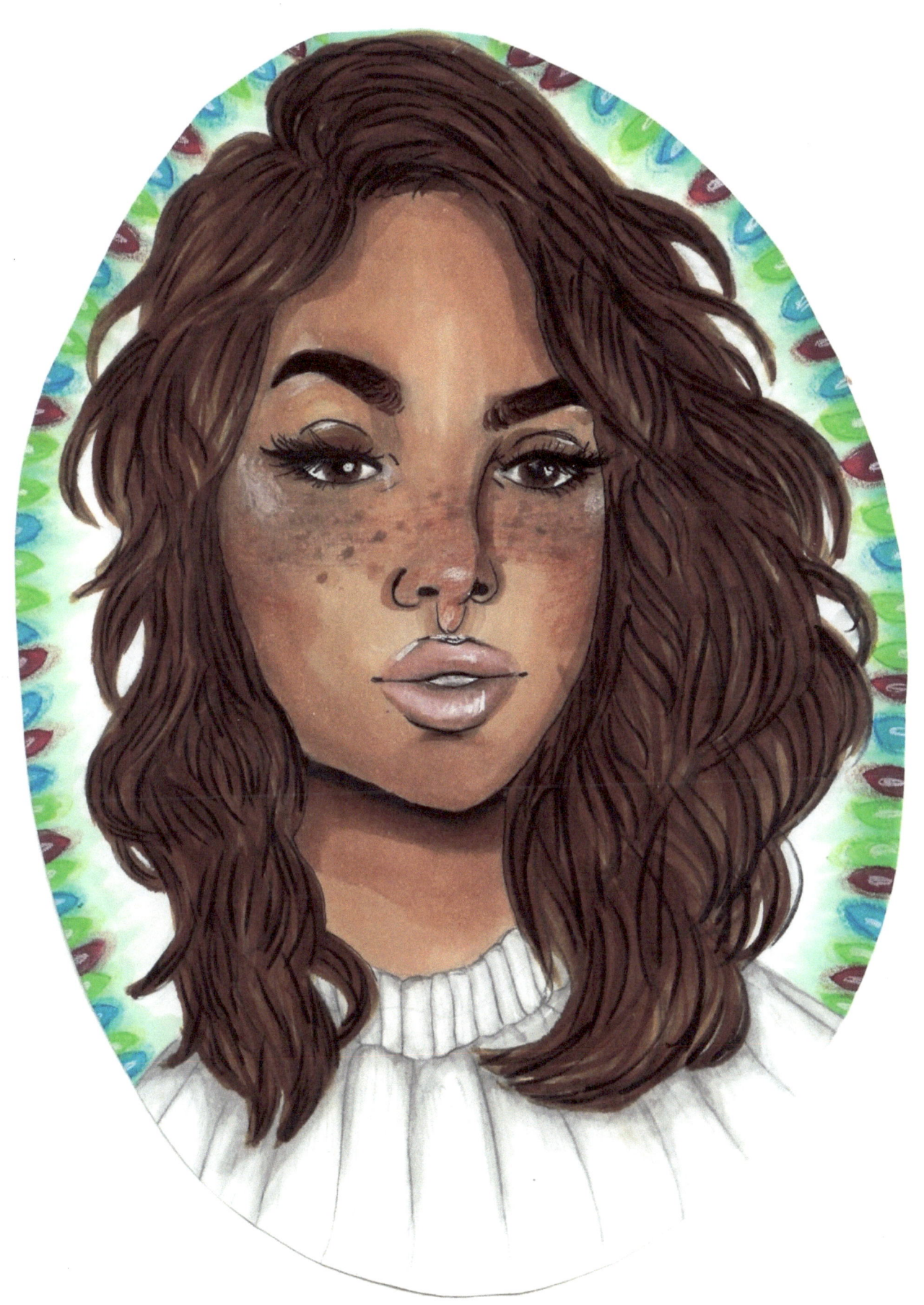

2018

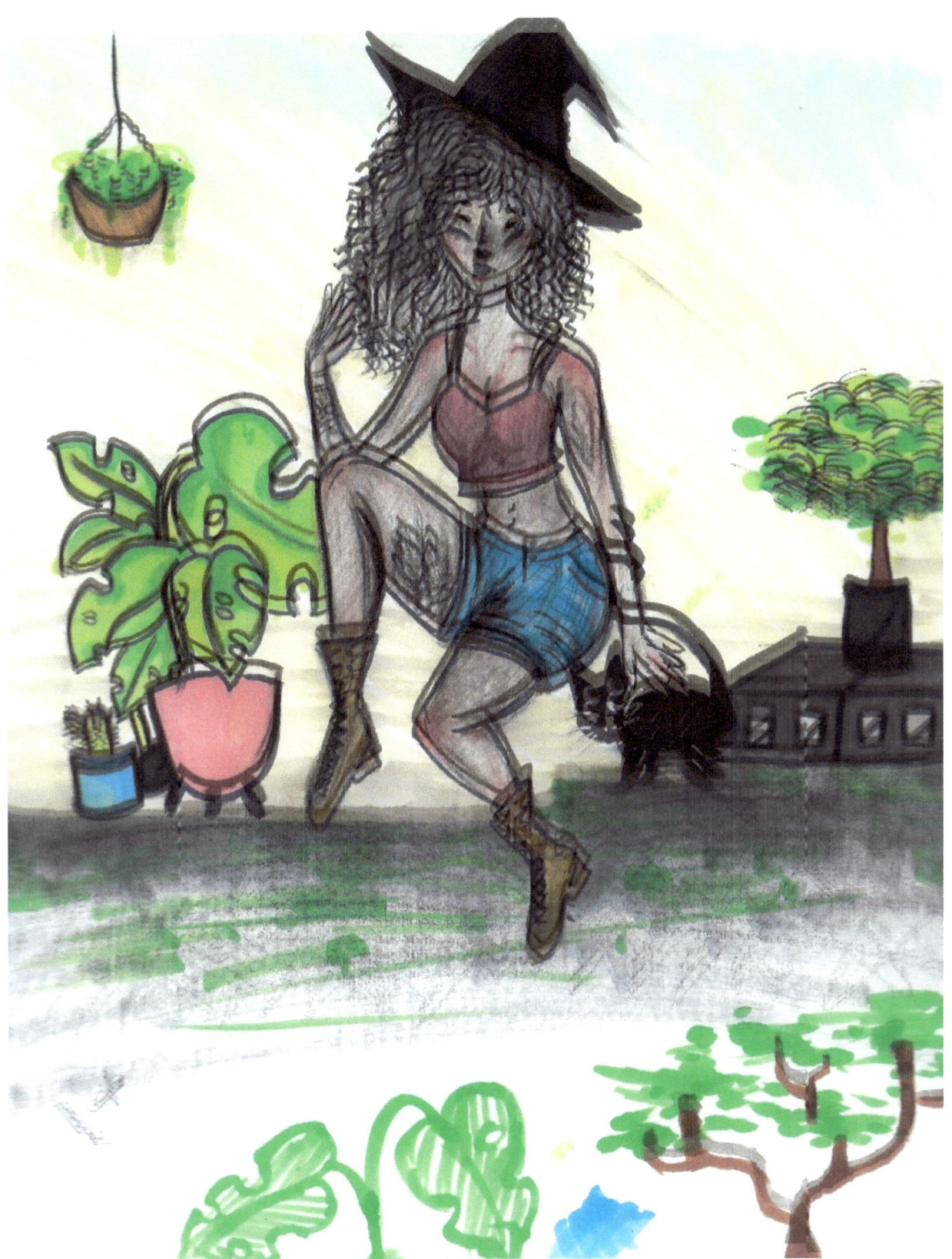

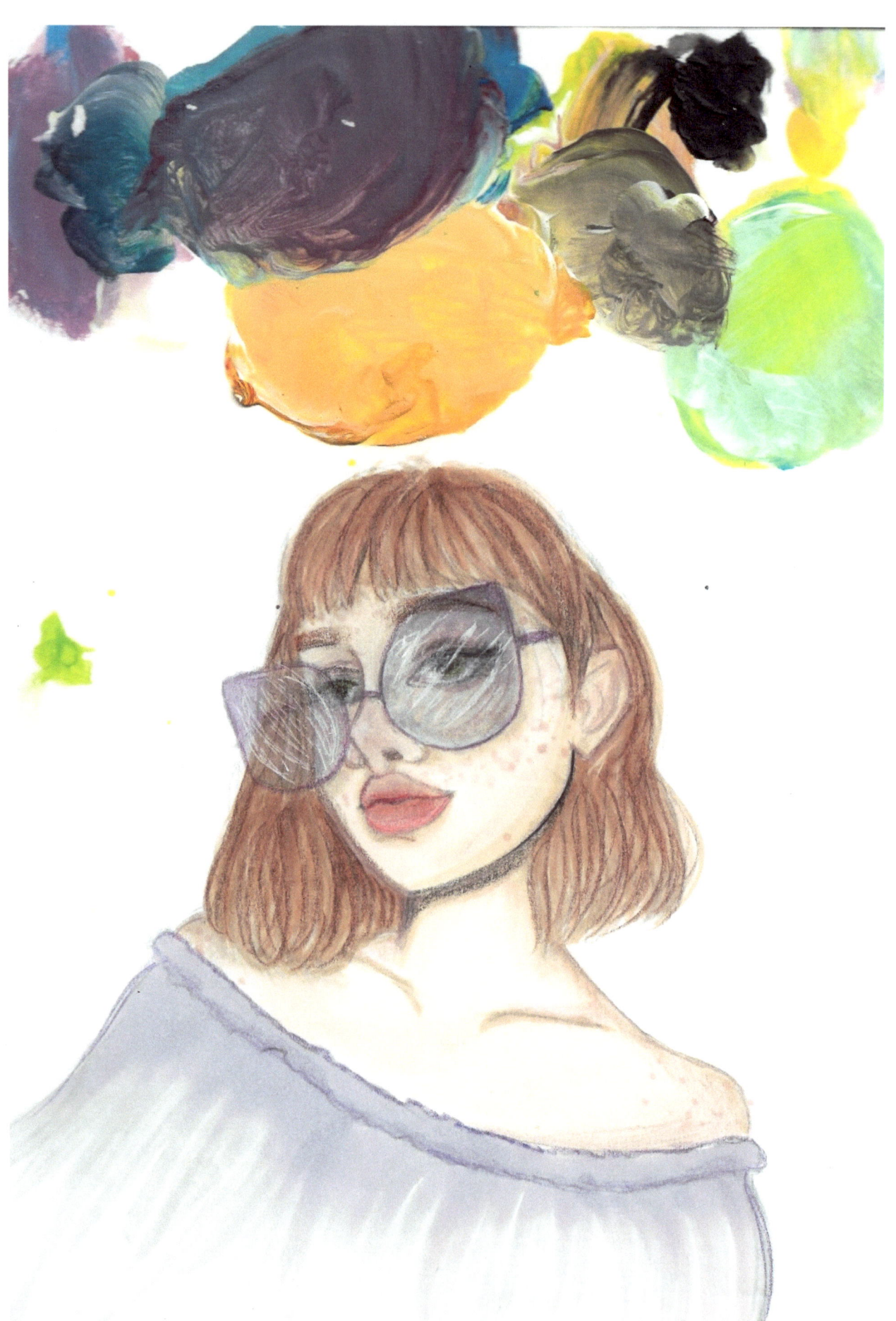

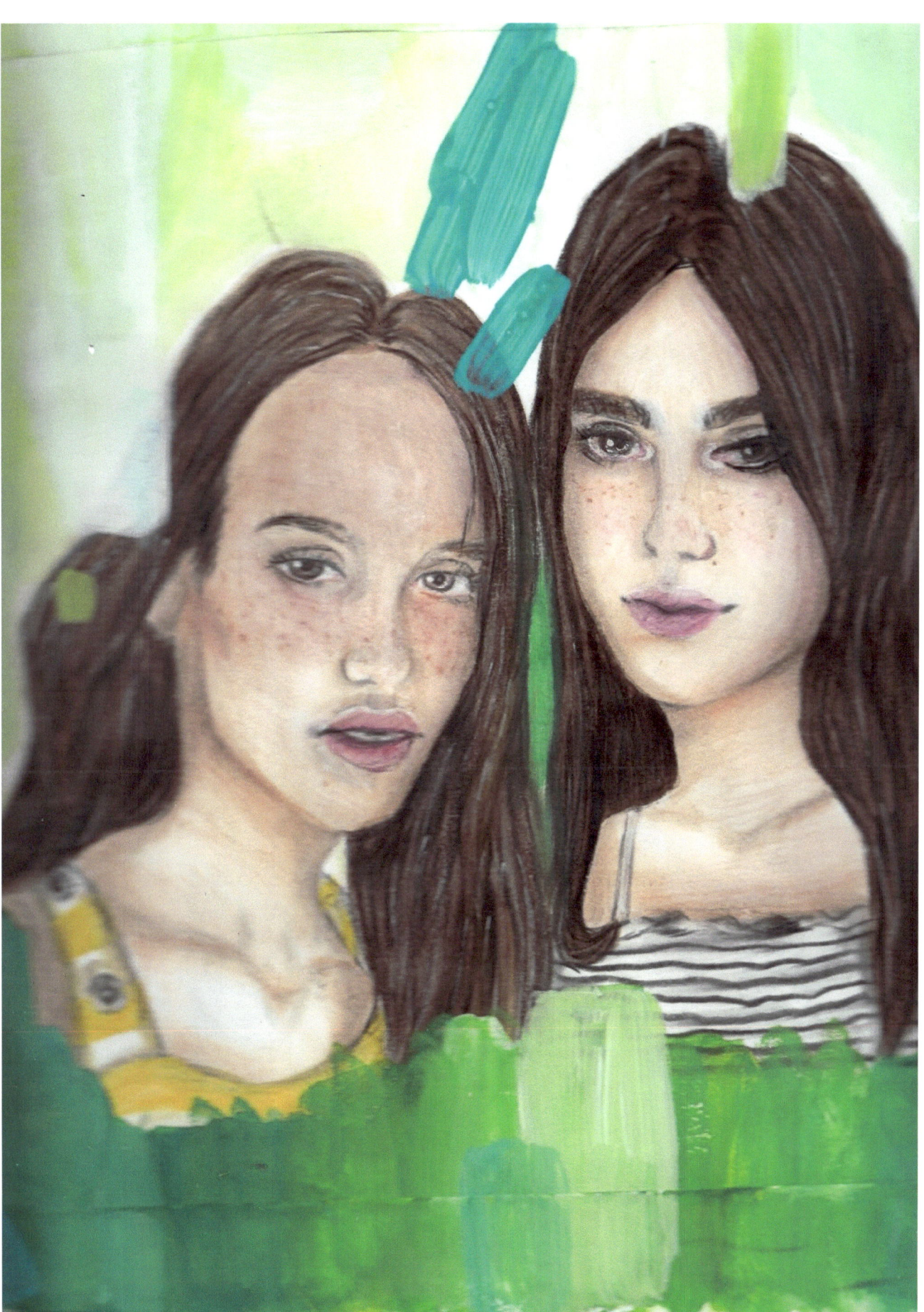

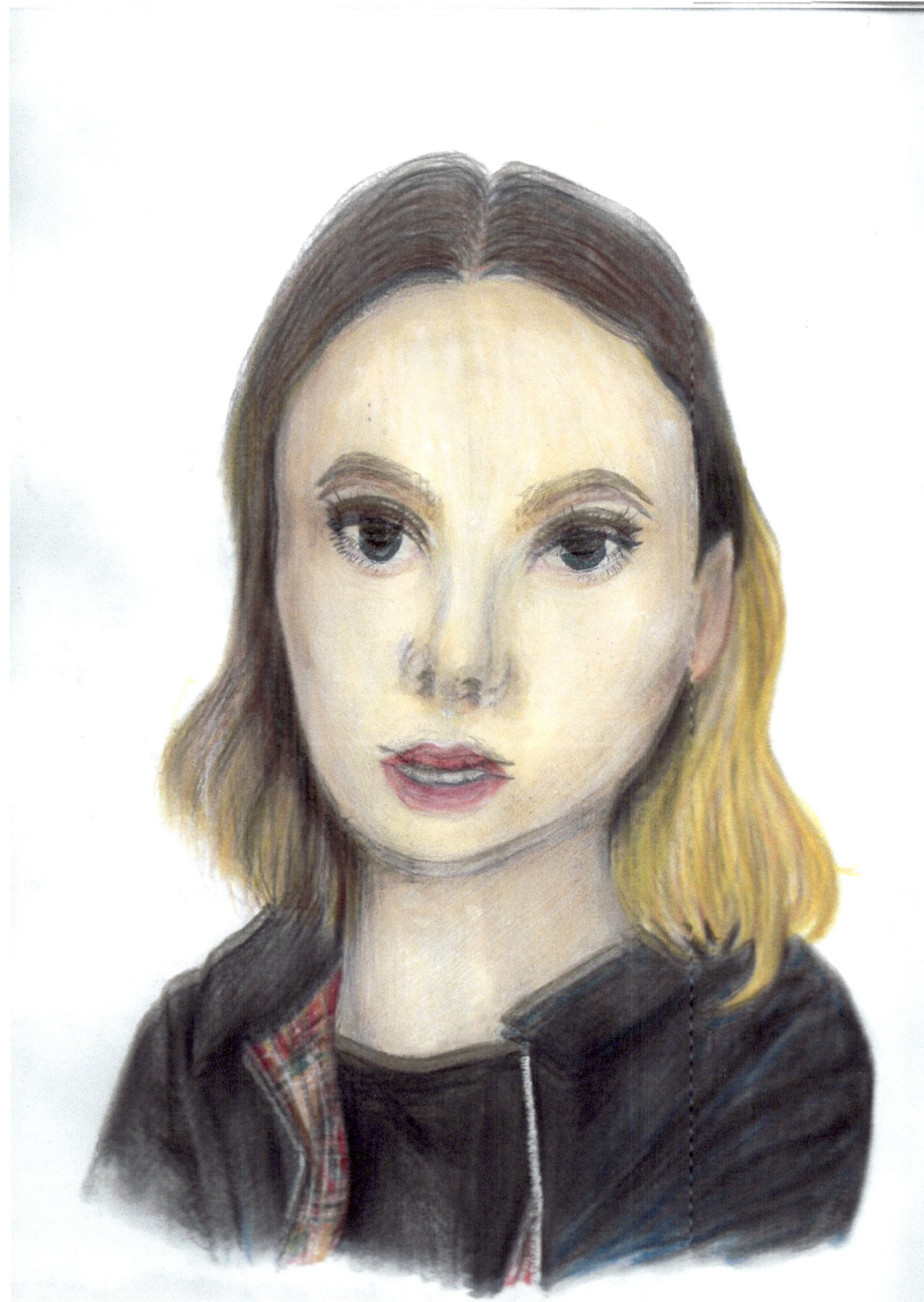

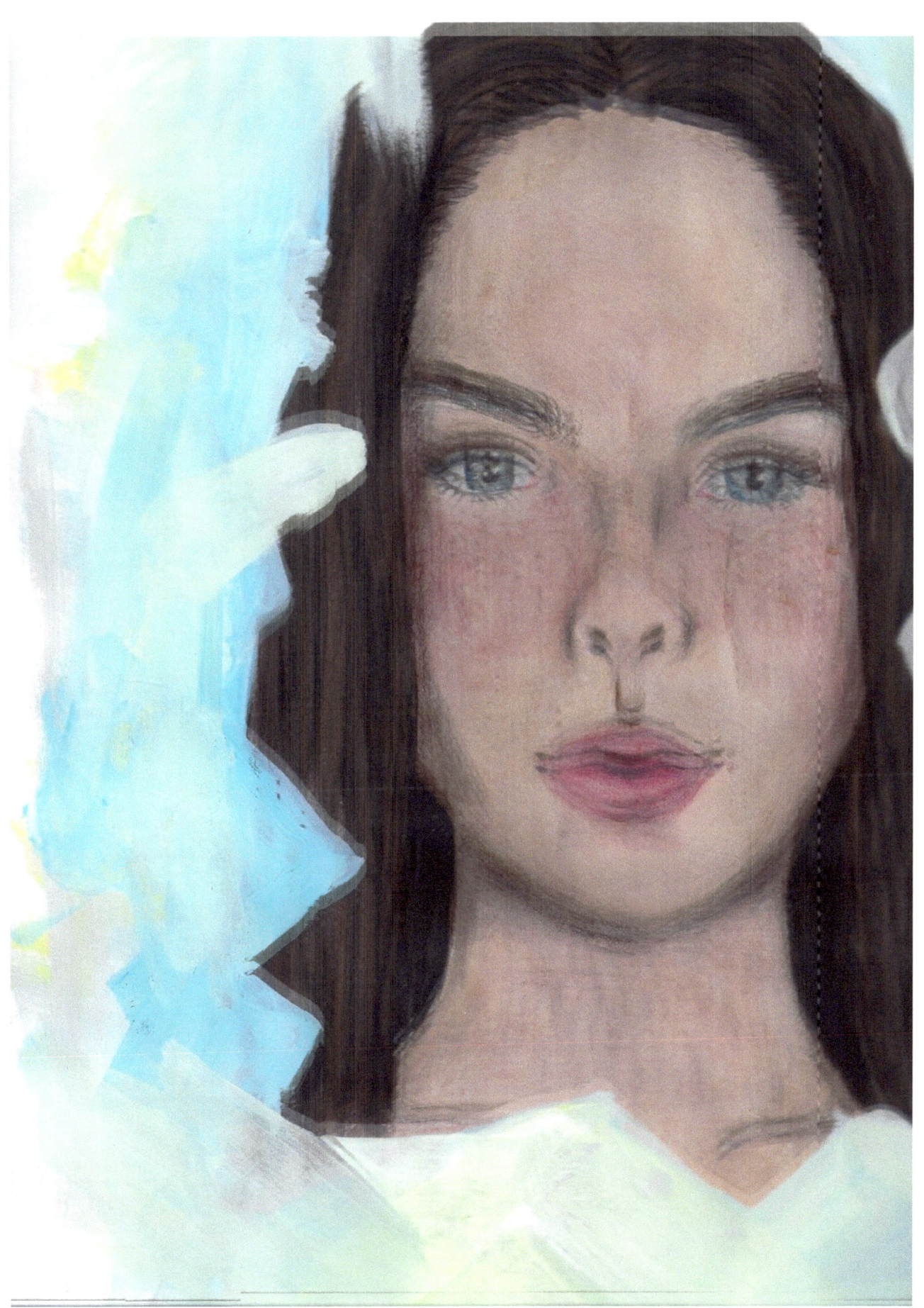

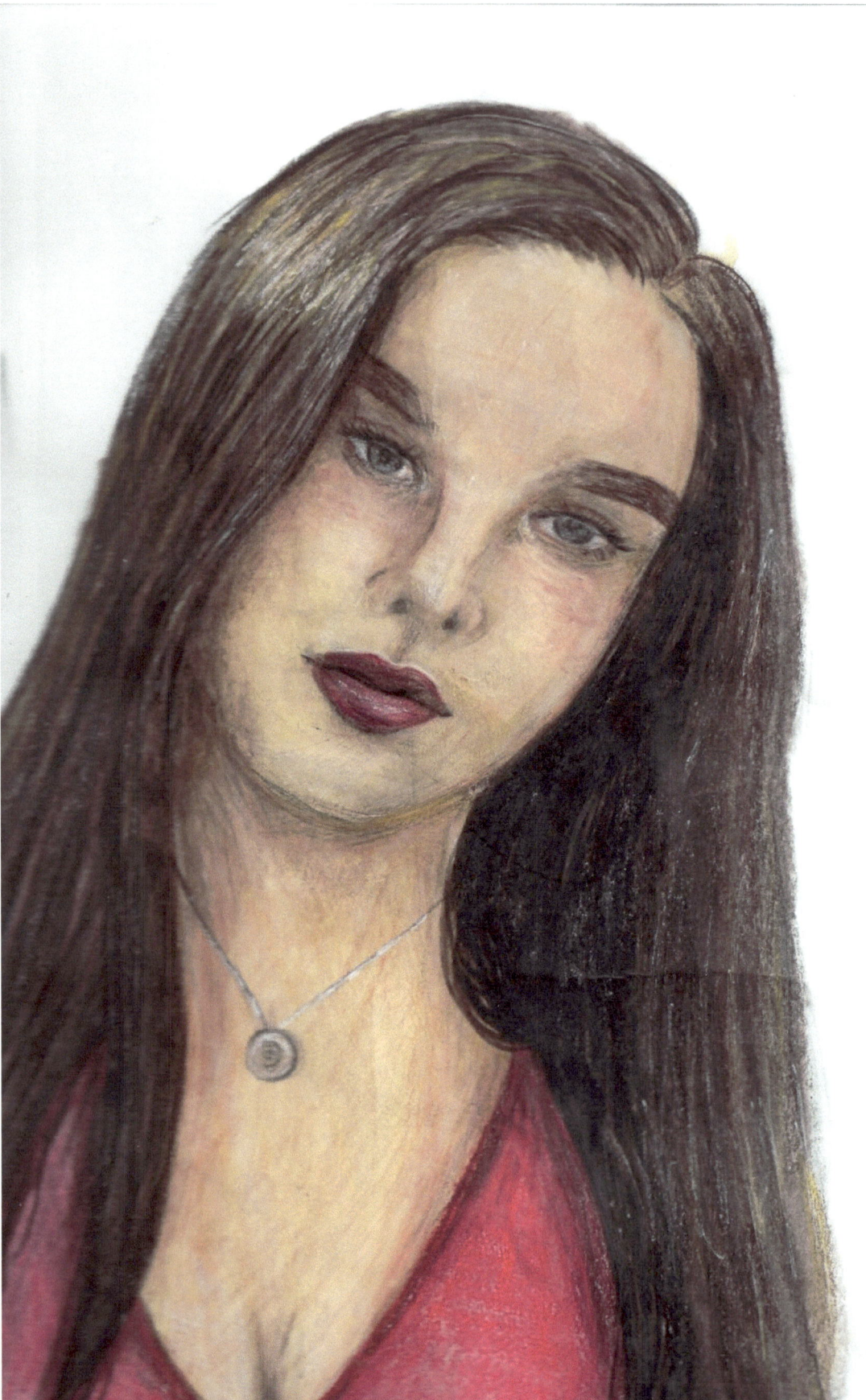

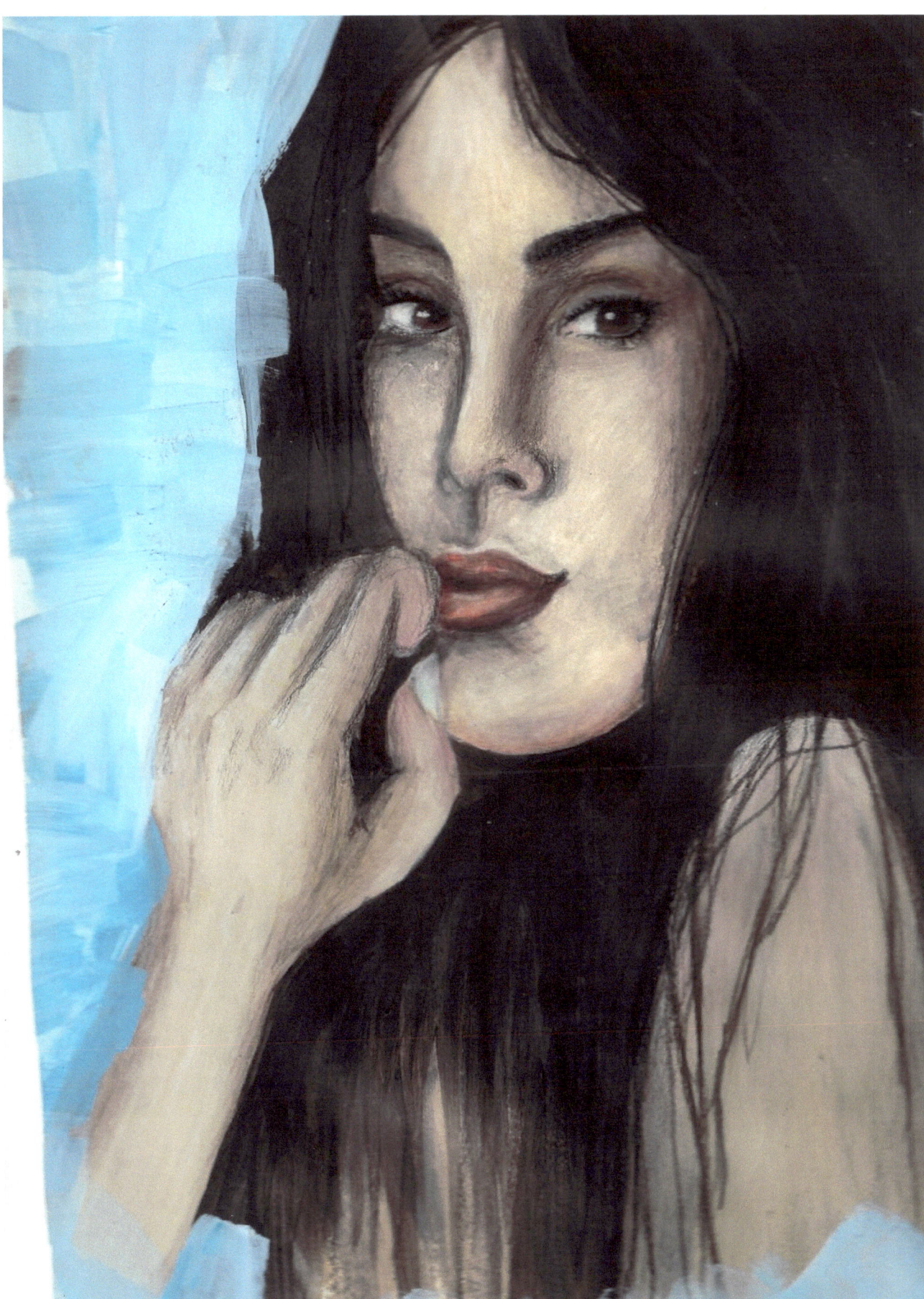

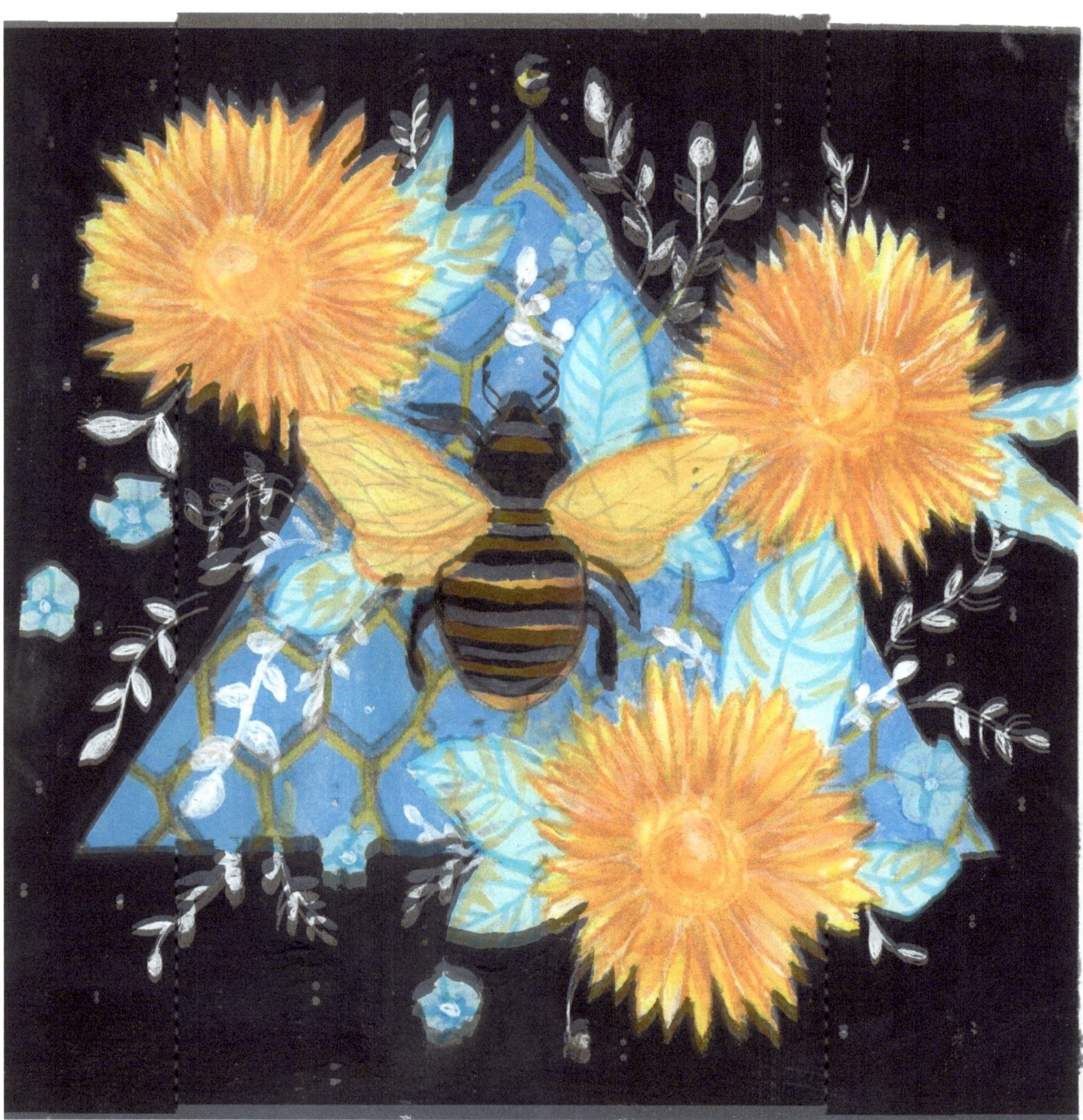

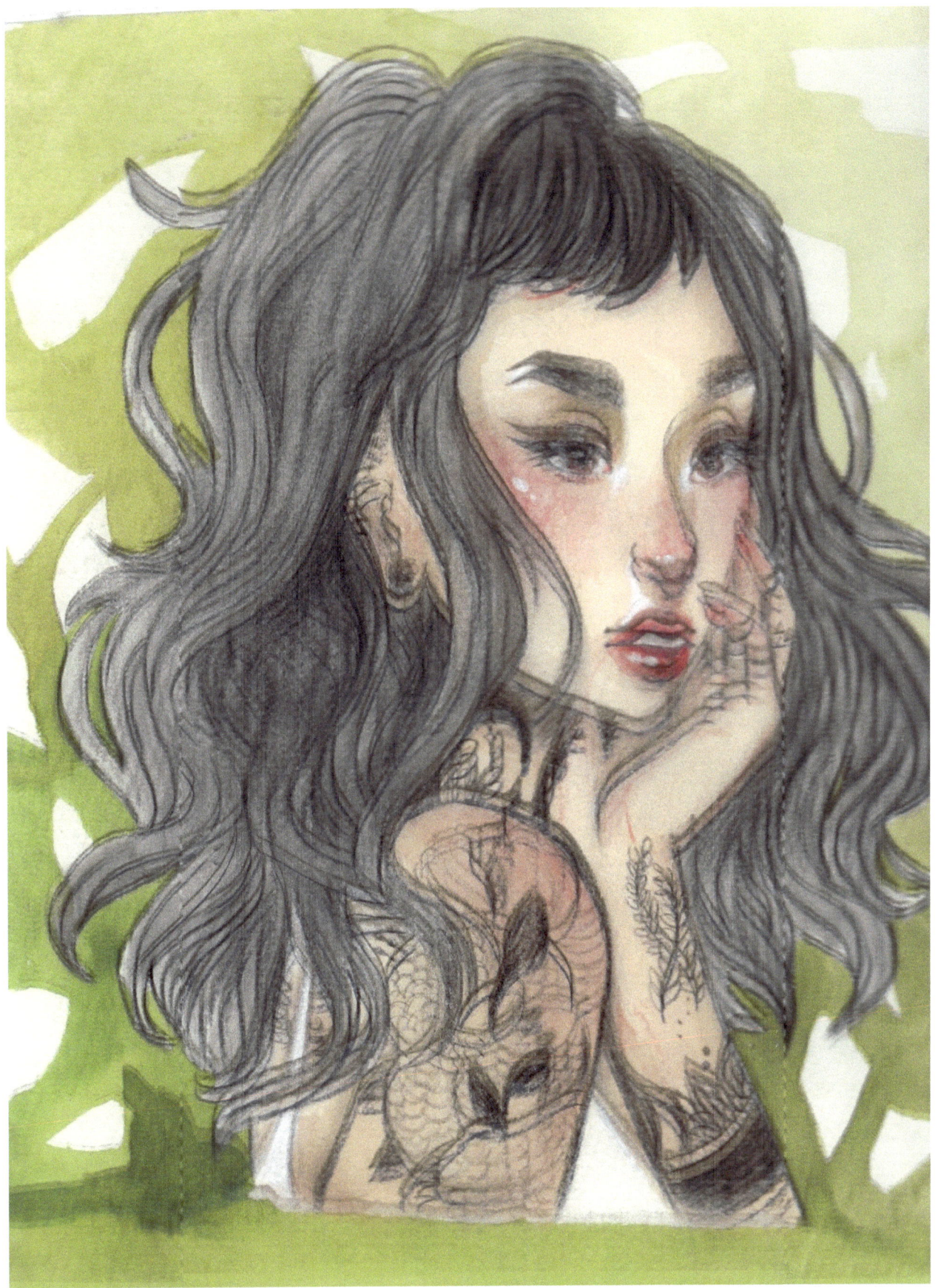

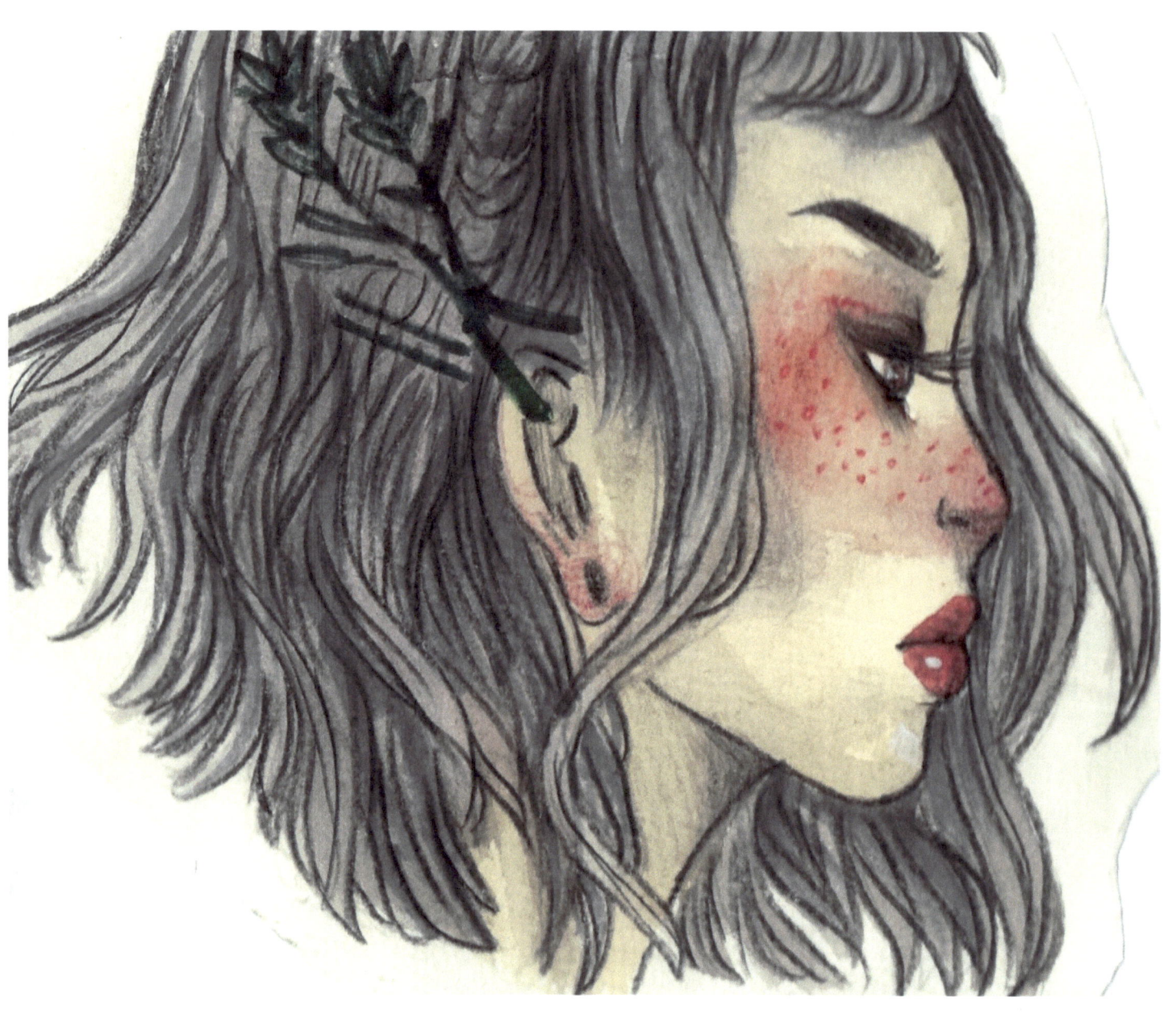

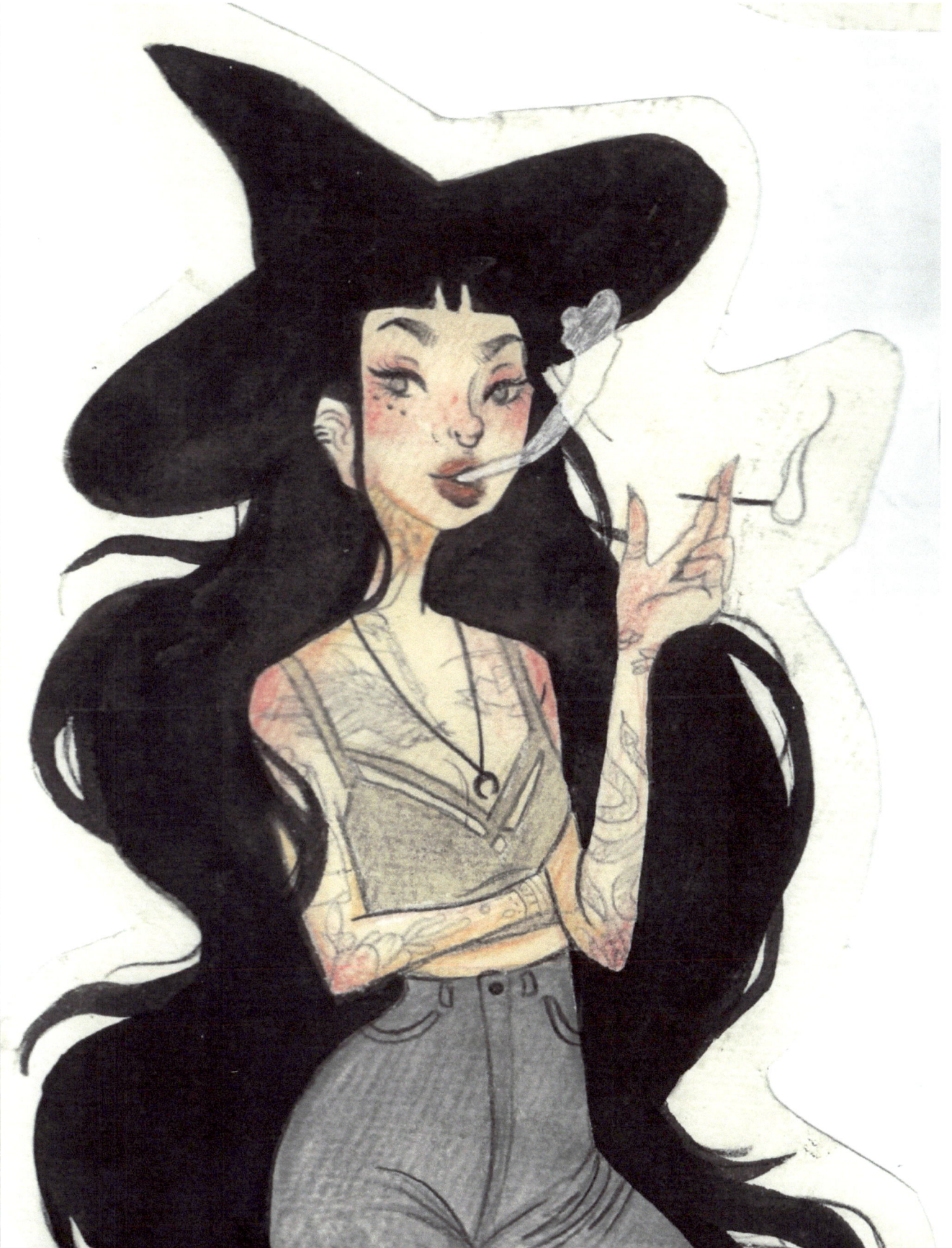

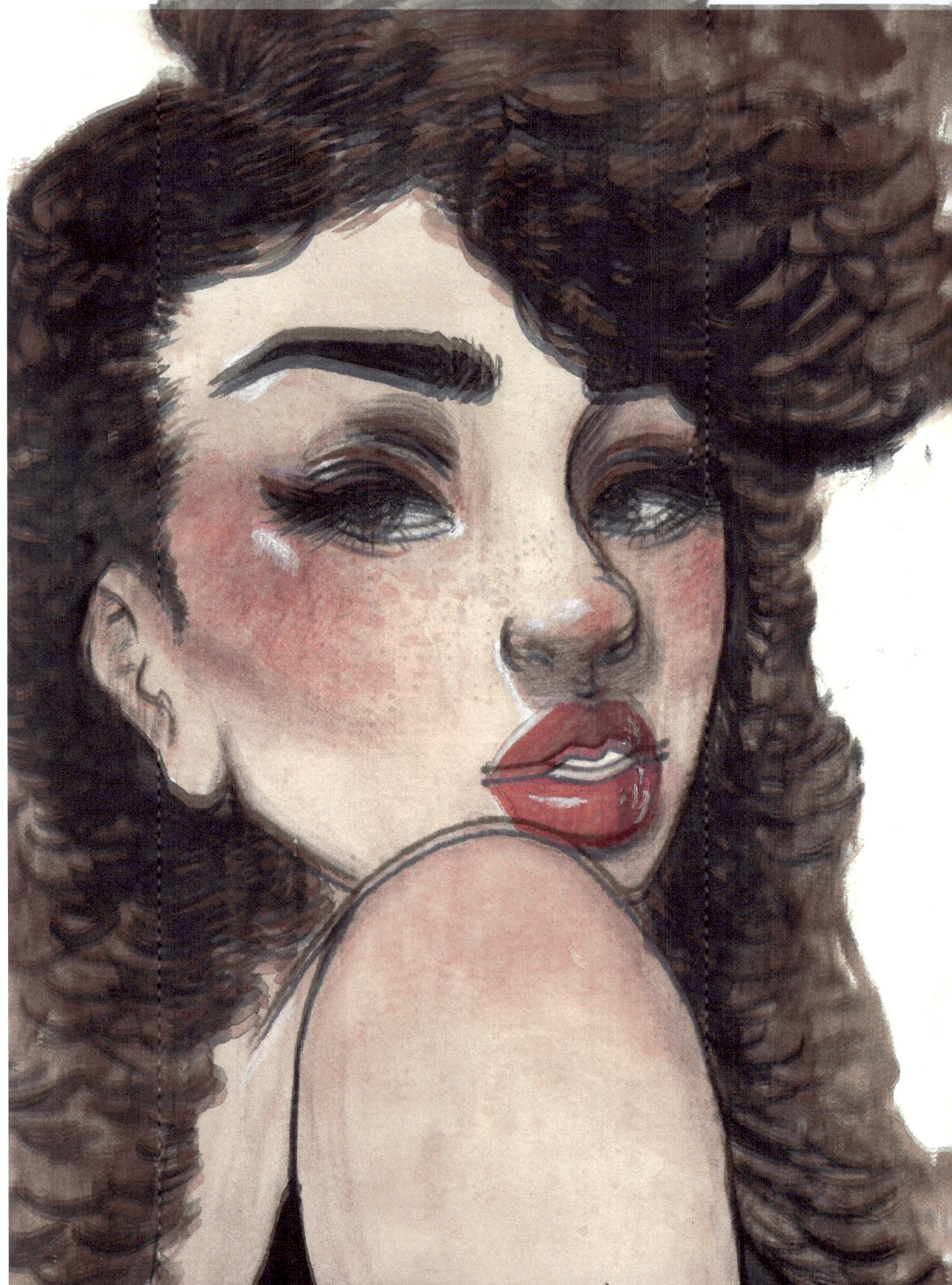

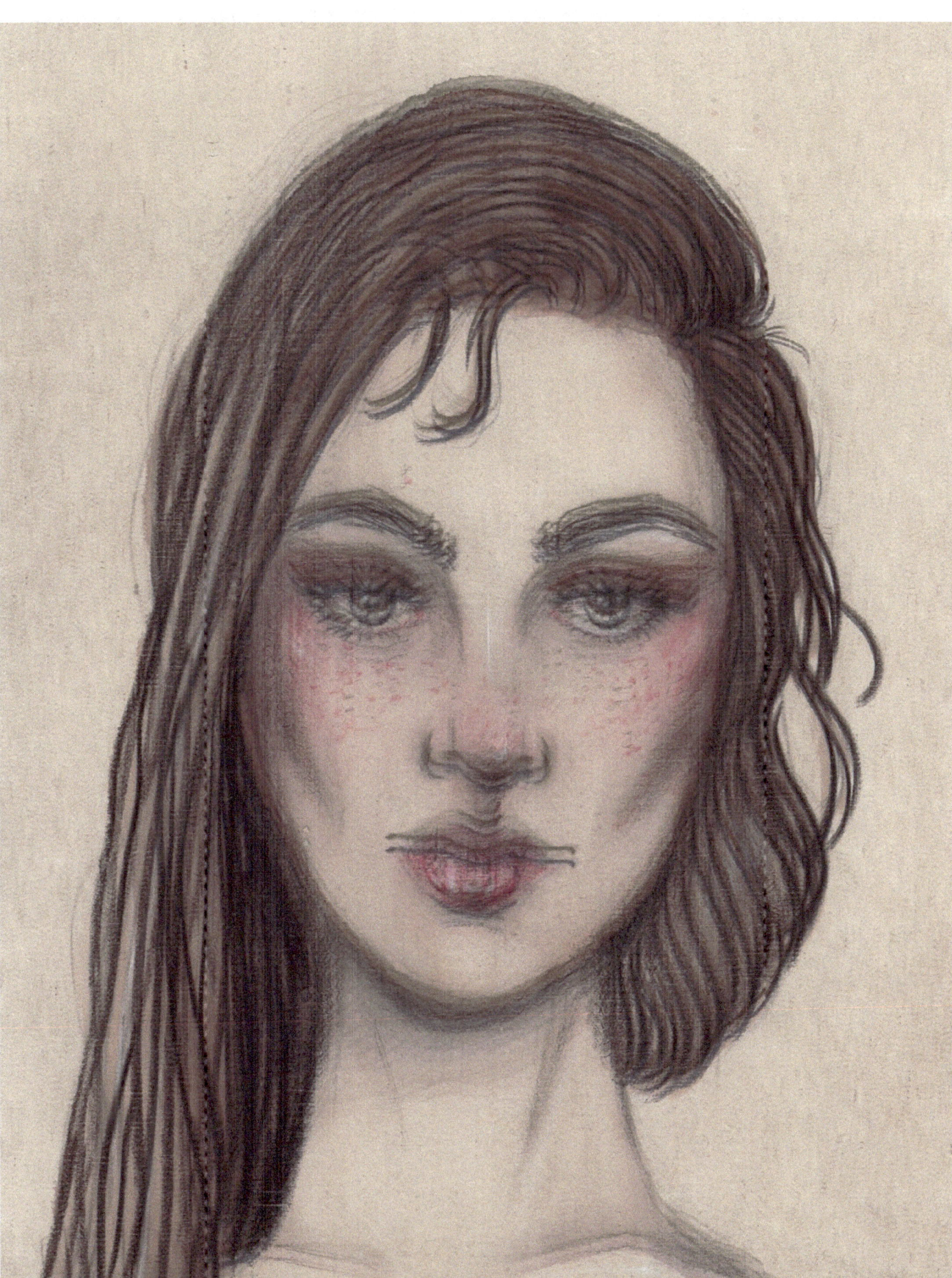

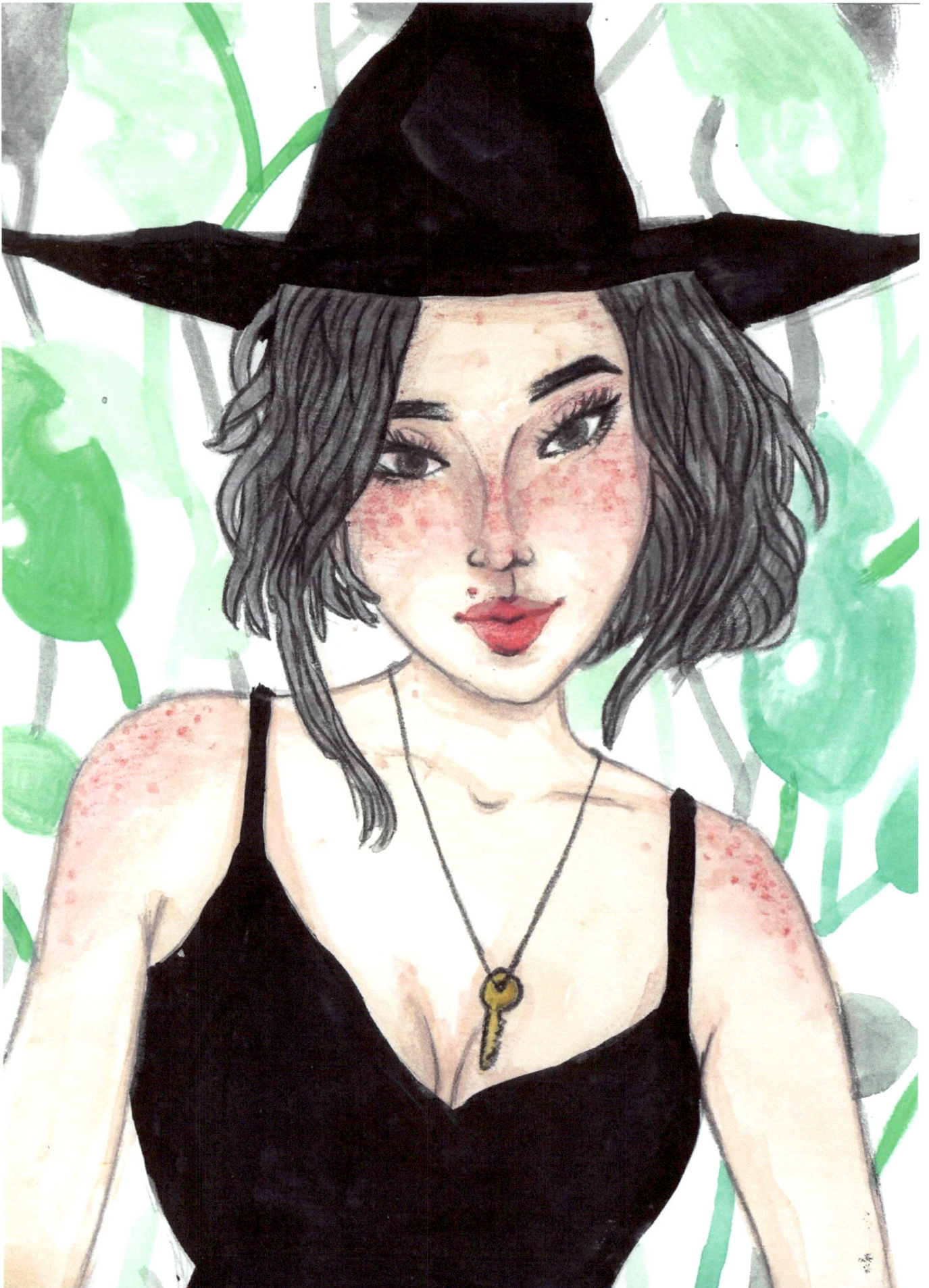